Some Wonderful

Some Wonderful

Heidi Watts

White River Press
Amherst, Massachusetts

Copyright 2022 Heidi Watts

All rights reserved.

Published by White River Press, Amherst, Massachusetts
whiteriverpress.com

ISBN: 978-1-935052-88-3

Any photo credits not credited elsewhere are courtesy of the Watts family. All illustrations are courtesy of Linda Rubinstein.

Design credit: Emily Anderson. Original cover photo courtesy of Michael Herbert. Back cover photo courtesy Jimmy Karlin.

Library of Congress Cataloging-in-Publication Data

Names: Watts, Heidi, 1931- author.
Title: Some wonderful / Heidi Watts.
Description: Amherst, Massachusetts : White River Press, [2022] | Includes bibliographical references.
Identifiers: LCCN 2022017147 | ISBN 9781935052883 (paperback)
Subjects: LCSH: Watts, Heidi, 1931- | Middle Island (N.S.)--Social life and customs. | Middle Island (N.S.)--Anecdotes. | Subsistence fishing--Nova Scotia--Middle Island.
Classification: LCC F1039.L9 W38 2022 | DDC 971.6092 [B]--dc23/eng/20220518
LC record available at https://lccn.loc.gov/2022017147

CONTENTS

INTRODUCTION
    Some Wonderful 1

FAMILY STORIES
    A Hard Lookin' Old Place 7
    That First Summer 15
    Black T'ick a' Fog 25
    Birds and Beasts on Middle Island 29
    The Tide and I 35

FISHERMEN STORIES
    The Shop on Bell's Island 39
    The Slacker 45
    The Black Hirtles 53
    Bound to Happen 57

ESSAYS
    No Trusts Without Trust 67
    Who Hears the Fishes When They Cry? 73
    EPILOGUE 79
    Acknowledgements 83
    A Note About Illustrations 85
    REFERENCES & ENDNOTES 87

Map of LaHave Islands

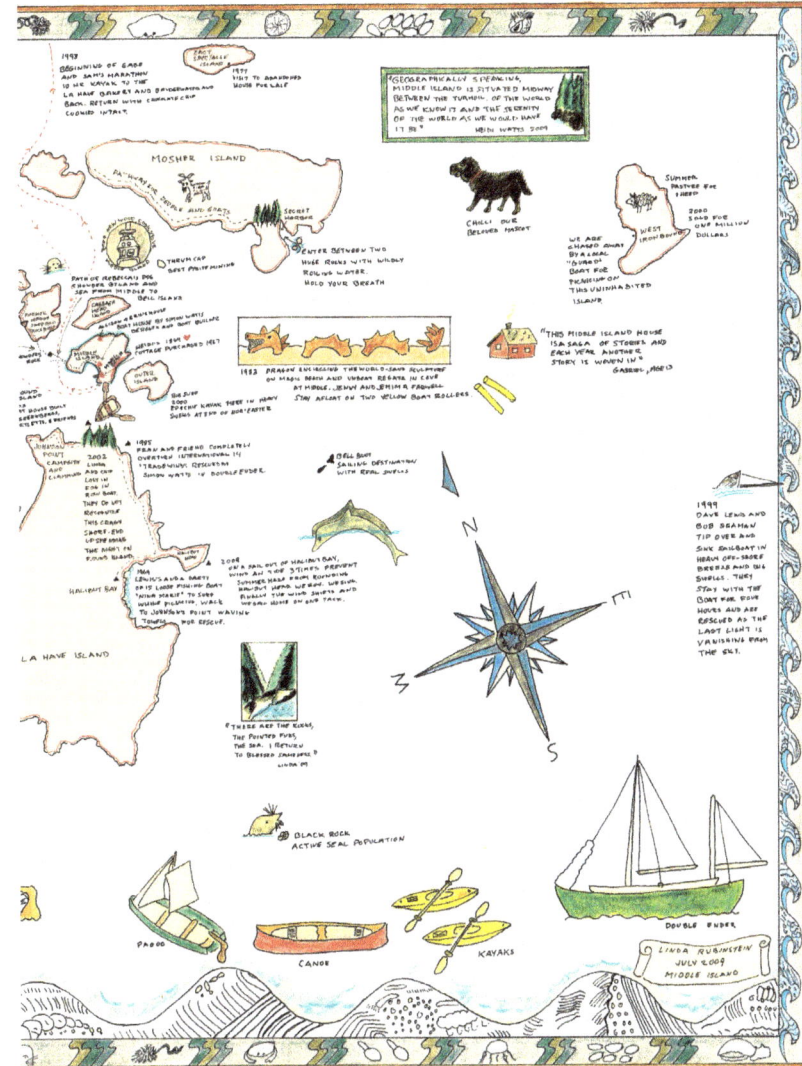

Ernest and Vera Baker, fomer residents of Middle Island. (Courtesy of LaHave Islands Maritime Museum.)

INTRODUCTION

Some Wonderful

"It's some wonderful how things has grow'd up on this island," Ernest Baker said, pushing his cap to the back of his head. Ernest Baker, 80 years old now, had been born and raised on Middle Island, a small island in an archipelago of islands at the mouth of the LaHave River just off the coast of Nova Scotia. If you were to sail due east from the last island, appropriately named Outer Island, eventually you would see the coast of Portugal.

My family had been spending our summers on Middle Island for thirty or forty years when we invited Ernest and his wife, Vera, to walk around the island and then have tea with us. We started with the "store" behind the house. Every proper fisherman's cottage needs a "store" to keep nets, tools, fishing equipment, boats and motor gear; sails to repair and herring in barrels slowly turning into fish oil—not a pleasant fragrance. The fish store was literally a "store" for gear, trade, tackle and trim.

With Ernest and Vera we walked along the shore, from the fish store to the boathouse—our addition—a big wooden structure for building and storing boats with a pleasant room upstairs for guests. My husband, Simon, was a boat builder; the boat house was filled with boats he had made; a lapstrake rowboat named Sea Urchin, the replica of a Cornish fishing boat, Silver Thread, and another replica, an International 14, always referred to as 'The Fourteen.'

On a map, our cove looked like a cookie with a bite taken out of it. We walked across the sandy beach which created the inner curve of the bite, poked around in the ruins of John Berrigan's house—"A fine big house, mind you, pity it come down," and through the woods to the other side where you could see the remains of an old breakwater and the three remaining houses, one as old as our own, the other two built around the turn of the century. The far side, facing north and the open ocean has a rock bound coast, difficult for scrambling over, so we turned east and walked through the interior of the island on what was known as "The Road" although now it was a mixture of bog, bush, scrub, rocks and stunted trees. As the sea became visible so did a small freshwater pond, then a little bluff and the foundations of two old houses, one on a rock foundation, the other on crumbling concrete, telling the story of two generations of Bakers, and the changing history of the island. We sat on the wall of the concrete foundation, the newer house, and Ernest told us the story of taking the house down and moving it to Bell Island where there was better access to the mainland, more people, churches and a school.

Ernest had with him a picture of his present house on Bell Island and a picture of the house which had been here. He grinned at us and said, "How you 'spose we ever got it in from Middle Island to Bell?"

We looked appropriately mystified and curious. He continued:

> We took out all the windows and the doors, just sawed 'em out and we went to work, and they sawed this away from the house (pointing to one side of the house in the picture) and they sawed the roof away from the house, and they sawed down here (pointing to another part of the picture) and yew! They done the same to the rest of the house. The roof was in four pieces and the sides was the same.
>
> You know what a double dory is then? Well, then we brought double dories in and the young fellers, and the boys, and everybody helped and got it down to the shore and put it across the dories, like that, you understand (gesturing with his hands). Everybody was to help the next feller, yew! And, we brought it in and carried it up to where it is now. Oh, dear! Right where it is now, and put it together, put everything together again, exact like it stood out on Middle Island.

Vera added her part: "That house wasn't very crooked. And all that it had been through and everything! I papered quite a lot of those rooms and it wasn't very crooked. I bet you that the new houses are not as straight."

We swung our legs sitting on the edge of the concrete foundation and looked over the Outer Island Gut to Outer Island at about the same elevation, and imagined a collection of double dories, and a large gathering of men in the dories, on the sand and in the water, manhandling the side of a house across the thwarts of the dories and rowing away with it.

This was a narrow gut—we liked to swim between the islands—and the beach below was one of the most beautiful beaches on the LaHave Islands, affectionately named "Magic Beach" by our children. The sand was clean, a greyish white with a patch of rocks good for climbing on or sitting against; small, stunted green-blue spruce created a background. The sun rose and fell in an opening between the two islands; we saw many gorgeous sunrises through the gap, as I suppose Ernest and his siblings had done as children. We completed the trip by walking down the beach, through the woods, past another rock foundation covered in moss, and coming at last to the promised tea in our house, in a kitchen Ernest and Vera knew well from another time and another family.

What Ernest meant when he remarked on what had "growed up" on Middle Island were the trees, the bushes, and the buildings, but to that cascade of images I added my family, my children, myself—blessed by all we had learned of living close to the land and the water; of all we had learned of a culture in radical transition.

From time to time over the 50 years we spent on Middle Island, I kept a journal, wrote long letters to distant friends and relations, interviewed fishing families and recorded fishing stories. These stories are a small selection of all that paper, coaxed out of files, excavated from the computer, and brought to the light of day. I wanted to celebrate the beauty of the islands, the land, and the sea—and I wanted the honor of being welcomed into a way of life which evolved over 150 years and disappeared in less than 50. This is a celebration of what is, and a lament for what is lost. I watched with pain, close-up and personal, the increasing destruction and final death of the fisheries. Fifty years is a very short time to destroy a large and vital piece of our environmental heritage.

In 1967 you could drop a hook in the water and bring up a cod. In 2021 most off-shore commercial fishing is regulated; you might bring up one fish on your hook but not two, and with the fish the terns are gone, the tide pools empty, and the houses too. The loss of a livelihood means the loss of a community. Now on the islands, there are just a few old men and women with their pictures and their memories, and the summer people who come and go.

I also wanted to capture for you and for myself the beauty of the sea, sand, sky, and rocks—what was unique in the culture of the time and place, and the inevitability of change.

As we were pulling these Nova Scotia stories our of the files and off the blog I realized we had another, simultaneous collection to draw from: the sketches and drawings made by my dear friend, Linda Rubenstein. Linda, with her husband Chip, visited me on the islands almost every summer for weeks at a time. We had many island exploring adventures together and some great meals. When we weren't in a boat, on a beach or at the kitchen stove Linda was drawing, sketching, painting. Chip was repairing boats, houses, docks, and inventing improvements. Linda's drawings add richness, texture and another perspective on the islands we love.

I dedicate this book to those who shared those experiences, both good and bad, with me: my family, my friends from afar, and my friends from the islands. It couldn't have happened without you.

July 24 Lupine Pods

July 18 Round Island, Brilliant Sunshine

Cove Island house before painting with cod-liver oil. (Courtesy of Michael Herbert.)

FAMILY STORIES

A Hard Lookin' Old Place

It was a fine morning in June when I stood at the door of a large white house, stern and foursquare, overlooking the Lewis' cove.

I looked out upon a serene blue sea, an ethereal blue with little sparkles as the sun glinted off a pattern of small perky wavelets. The sea stretched out as far as I could see, dotted with small and smaller clusters of small and smaller islands. Turning my head to the right, and then left, I could see clusters of tidy houses, all with docks and fishing boats along the shore.

It was 1966. I had been at the center of a controversy in the small rural town of Putney, Vermont, involving the local school and political climate which revealed a variety of conflicts over values, rights, responsibilities, and the role of people "from away." (I have written about this before, with "Communists, Pacifists and Aliens go Home" on my blog). After months of meetings, letters to the editor, arguments, and explanations exposing the underlying tensions between people "from away" and the long-term residents, my husband Simon and I were both exhausted.

As a final salvo in the conflict a school board member called me on a Sunday night in early June to say that school was closing a week early—that is to say, immediately—and intimated that he would be happy never to see me again. Within a few days, Simon's mother, Marjorie, arrived from England for a visit. Meanwhile, a board flew out of the planer backward breaking most of the bones in the back of Simon's hand. He came back from the doctor, his arm in a cast and a sling and demanded, gesticulating with the other: "Doesn't your sister have a house in Nova Scotia?"

"Well, yes," I said, "I think they bought it about two years ago."

"Let's go," he said, and walked out again.

I called my sister Fran and her husband Dave Lewis. They said they would be delighted to lend us their house for a few weeks in June and would call their local fishing friends, Collin and Kathleen, to open the house. Collin could also pick us up at the government wharf since there was no way to get to Bell's Island in 1964 without a boat.

In less than a week, Simon had hitched his sailboat—a "Comet" which he shared with a friend—to the back of our Volkswagen pickup truck and we were off, Marjorie and Simon in the front. In the back, under the canvas hood which made the truck resemble a covered wagon, me and the two children, Richard and Alison, ages six and three, were bedded down on mattresses. I was feeling distinctly ill and began to suspect that there was, as Marjorie suggested, a bun in the oven.

In a pattern which became a part of every succeeding summer, we left home after supper and drove the eight or nine hours it took to get to Bar Harbor. This was before the Maine turnpike, before the interstate, before the beckoning motel. We arrived at Bar Harbor in time to drive to the top of Acadia Mountain for the sunrise, ready to board the Bluenose Ferry at seven a.m.

Eight hours later, the Bluenose docked in Yarmouth and we slowly made our way over the two-lane road which wound through the fishing villages fringing the southern coast of Nova Scotia. This was also before the provincial highway, Route 103. On this occasion, when we got to Bridgewater—a 30-minute drive to the islands—we left Alison with her grandmother at a hotel and the three of us set about trying to find the government wharf on Bush Island. I remember driving in the dark and the fog over a long narrow road with the sound of the sea on either side, as though we would soon drive right into it.

When we did see lights in the dark, they barely illuminated a large wharf with the dim shapes of boats and masts rocking slightly and rubbing in a now familiar way against the wooden pilings. The only people in sight were the dim shapes of a man and a woman, coming forward, smiling broadly, to introduce themselves. First Kathleen, "Simon? Heidi? Ah, Richard! And yes, Kathleen! Call me Aunty Kay." And then Collin, a large man in a fisherman's oilskins with huge hands and a warm smile.

We climbed down a long ladder into the void of what Collin called black t'ck a fog and shivered slightly in the damp, open boat. We were to learn that June in Nova Scotia is about the temperature of Putney in April.

My husband Simon described it like this:

> We were met at the breakwater by a local fisherman, Collin Hirtle, with his wife, Kathleen, and his lobster boat, the June R. I realized

later that bringing a boat that size down a narrow, winding channel at night—and on a falling tide—was quite a trick. There were no navigation lights and some of the few channel markers had a red plastic glove stuck on top with the thumb pointing ahead. So a stranger was left to guess on which side to pass."

Collin started up the engine, while Kathleen chattered away with questions and assertions of help, and by some miracle, or so it seemed, he steered us through the cloud of damp, impenetrable darkness until we came to another dock. There, we unloaded ourselves and our luggage, and crept up a long path to a house recognizable that dark night only by the lights in its windows. Even better, when we got inside a fire in the big wood stove was pushing back the waves of chill and reaching out to us in full promise of hospitality.

Had we been delivered blindfolded we could not have had less sense of where we were. The primary clues that night came from the other senses: the sound of a soft light wind and of the sea (more a murmur than a crash on that quiet night), the tangy smell of the water, the hemlocks we later discovered behind the house, dusty rooms, and wood smoke.

Soon after a bottle of rum appeared. Collin, grinning broadly, was passing out the glasses and then the bottle. The ultimate in island hospitality was to invite the guest to pour his own drink, a way of saying take as much as you want: "What's mine is yours."

We awoke to a calm Mediterranean-blue sea with the sun glinting off perky wavelets. While I went into Bridgewater to rescue Marjorie and Alison, Simon and Richard went exploring.

We spent the next ten days reveling in the absence of human strife and absorbed with watching the colors of the sea change, the variety of shore and land birds, and meeting the neighbors. Simon, with his hand in a cast, put his boat in the water and sailed off. He met all the local fisherman for whom, at this time, a new face and a foreigner was a sight to cherish, and he mapped in his mind the layout of the LaHave Islands, their houses, and their inhabitants. We often spent the evenings with Collin and Kathleen, listening to fisherman's stories, and every day I took the children over to visit Aunty Kay. Collin and Kathleen had two adopted children, Wade, who went fishing with his father whenever he wasn't in school, and Mary Anne, who helped with the domestic chores. Collin was known as a good fisherman and Kathleen as a force to be reckoned with.

A few days before we left, Simon came back from one of his sailing expeditions and announced, "I have found the house for us!"

I didn't know we were looking for a house.

"It's in a perfect location, with a dock and store." (In island vernacular a small barn where bait and fishing gear were stored). "It's empty but I am going to find out who owns it and buy it."

In the 20 or so years since the end of World War II, social reforms in Canada brought unemployment insurance, pensions, fishing subsidies, and a health insurance scheme while at the same time war production and manpower were redirected to domestic needs. Most of the double-ended sailing boats with oars and sails now supplemented with simple single-cylinder engines—"putt-putt's," as we called them—and then double-cylinder engines.

In 1966, almost everyone was motoring to the fish in the sailing boats with an engine of some kind. Purpose-built fishing boats with boat motors came later. Technological changes brought radar, sonic depth finders, and two-way radios which made fishing safer and more productive. No longer dependent on sails and oars, the fishermen did not need to be on the outer islands and began to move closer to roads, hospitals, schools, and shops. Often the houses they left were abandoned—"Who would want to live out there?"

On Middle Island in 1930, there were 10 houses. By 1960 there were only seven. By 1966 two more disappeared. The house that was to be ours was on its way to disintegration, and Walter Walfield, the old fisherman who owned it had moved into his dead brother's house, closer to the remaining occupied house and a better dock. He was delighted to be able to get money for the house to pay the debts from his wife's funeral: $200.

As Simon described it:

> I came around a rocky point on Middle Island and saw a house that I knew immediately would make an ideal summer house for us. It had that neglected look that unoccupied dwellings acquire—shingles missing and a few roof tiles that had been crudely repaired with flattened tin cans. Also a ruinous dock with an impossibly steep slip. So I asked around and found that the owner, Walter Walfield, had moved into his brother's house on the far side, the more sheltered side, of Middle Island. When I found him and asked if he'd consider selling the house, he seemed taken aback that anyone would want 'such a hard-looking old place,' but he agreed to sell me the house and land and asked if $200 would be too much.

Simon and Walter went to Bridgewater to see a lawyer and sign the deed, but when Simon discovered there had been no title search he asked the lawyer to see to that, assuming the lawyer would make sure we had a clear title and then send us the completed document. Walter didn't understand what a "clear title" meant and was disappointed not to receive any money. Simon gave him $20 "for the furniture" and Walter went home content with a case of beer and a bottle of rum, precious commodities on the islands. Walter was not much of a drinker himself, but he had friends.

We left on another fine day in June, talking about when we would come, and what we would do next summer. I still had no idea what the house looked like inside or out.

But that is not the end of the story. We told everyone about our wonderful find, about the beauty and seclusion of the LaHave Islands, and the friendliness of the locals. I began to dream of being with three children on an island in the Atlantic during the long summer vacations.

In early September, Simon got a telephone call from Kathleen Hirtle, "Dr. McLetchie (a well-to-do doctor from New Hampshire who had been purchasing abandoned properties) is here and he is buying your house from Walter. If you want it you'd better come."

Simon put down the telephone and began throwing things into a suitcase. He was gone within the hour. By some fluke of providence, he arrived the next morning at the government wharf at the same time as Walter and the lawyer. Dr. McLetchie had offered Walter and the owner of the only other occupied house on Middle Island $500 and a bottle of rum. Simon insisted his claim on the property preceded Dr. McLetchie's as he had already engaged the lawyer (the same lawyer!) and paid a deposit of $20. Walter, who could not read or write, and who would sign the deed with a thumb print, did not understand the complications of deeds, titles, or deposits and was content to settle for the price of his wife's funeral. We did not know at the time how wise it was to insist on a title. Many of the island houses changed hands as the result of a grocery bill, a marriage, or the death of the old folks, which went unrecorded and made great complications in a later, more bureaucratic time.

Sometime in the winter, we got a copy of the deed for a house with a clear title, and the next summer I got my first chance to see the cottage. Standing on a rise of land near the entrance to a deep, rocky cove with a small sandy beach and a rapidly growing forest of hemlocks, it was as close to Paradise as I am likely to ever get.

We spent three weeks on Middle Island that summer, with Rebecca, three months old, sleeping in a bureau drawer, and the rest of us bunked out with mats and blankets on the floor. Our $20 worth of furniture consisted of a broken-down organ, a rocking chair tied together with fishing twine and two scruffy kitchen tables. Simon began re-shingling the roof, rescuing the foundation, and making the house livable. Then, as now, I found these physical challenges easier than the human ones.

Left to right: Kathleen, Heidi, Alison, Richard, Collin, Simon, Mary Anne in 1966. Front lawn of the Blue Hirtle's house on Bell Island.

That First Summer

I was unprepared for the beauty of a June day on the LaHave Islands. Old homesteads surrounded with perennials, daffodils waving bravely in a fierce wind; narcissus decorating stone outcroppings and perfuming the air, blooming lilacs drawing in as much of the surrounding land as they could manage in a year and slowly eating up the paths and fields around them and wood trails carpeted with four-petaled bunch berry, the white petals morphing into red berries by winter.

In fact, I was unprepared for just about everything that first summer in Nova Scotia. The previous year we had traveled by VW bus like a family of itinerant gypsies to stay in my sister's house on Bell's Island. Two small children, my English mother-in-law, and an increasingly difficult case of morning sickness. Simon had a broken wrist and his arm in a cast but managed, nonetheless, to put the small sailboat we were trailing behind the bus into the water and sail off single-handed (literally) to explore the islands. In a brief 10 days he found what he called "our house" and put a down payment on it before we had to come home. I never saw the house but loved the idea of a permanent home on these beautiful islands, the sea lapping softly in the background.

In June of the following summer, we loaded up the VW bus again, with one more child and without the mother-in-law. We set off for a house on an island without any public means of transport from the mainland. We did have an astonishing number of tools and the ubiquitous provisions. Our pediatrician friend, John Trumper, and his son, Peter, were to follow in a few days.

What were we thinking? I had never seen the house, Simon had seen it only from the outside. It was on a remote island without electricity and with only one other house, a derelict one, in sight. No one had lived in the house for several years. The roof leaked and the rock foundation, built in

1864, was sliding to its knees. Without electricity, there was no running water, no toilet. There was an outhouse, looking sturdier than the main house, built of boards three feet wide from the original timber on the islands. We found the well at the end of a long path through the woods by feeling for an indentation in the earth wholly hidden in ferns and bushes; a path created by thousands of footfalls by the "old people." In addition to the well there was one other essential amenity: an old cast-iron wood-fueled cook stove in the summer kitchen.

Although Simon had given Walter Walfield $20 for "the furniture," which neither he nor I had ever seen, and which turned out to be a small rocker with rails tied to each other by rope, two beaten-up wooden tables, an old foot-powered sewing machine, an even older and less serviceable organ, and one spool bed.

We gave the bed to our doctor friend when he arrived, and Simon hastily improvised three beds for Richard, Alison, and 10-year-old Peter. Rebecca, three months old, slept in a bureau drawer beside me on a mattress Simon found in the small, dark, grubby attic. We had brought with us a handsome mahogany bureau with brass handles, quite out of place but very serviceable, and three yellow kitchen chairs.

We only stayed three weeks that first summer, but in that time Simon managed to shore up the foundation and get new shingles on the roof. We cleared and cleaned and made lists of things to leave, things to bring, and things to do. We threw into the sea four barrels of stinking pickled salt herring hidden away in the "store," followed by the rusting remains of at least two previous wood cook stoves—pieces of old iron are still settling into the mud near the dock.

There was another house in the cove, facing ruin, as Simon wrote:

> Although built more recently, we had to let it go. It was a two story frame building, most of the glass still intact, and it was full of swallows. They nested precariously in curls of wallpaper as it slowly peeled off the plaster walls. At first, we used it as a source for firewood, then kindling until finally there was nothing left but rusty nails and plaster coated lath. I did meet a grandson of the original owner who described taking the path through the window to visit. 'A wonderful, good house,' he said. 'But no place to keep a boat—the wind laid onto it something wicked.'

We explored the island to find a magical, sandy beach on the northeastern side; a rapidly rotting old dock and breakwater on the south-western side of the island; and a freshwater pond very nearby. It took about 45 minutes to walk around or through the island, whether climbing over rocks along the coast or bushwhacking through the middle. I was in love with the islands but exhausted all the time. There were the three older children to be watched over, Rebecca to nurse, meals to be conjured up from a cranky wood stove I was struggling to learn to use, water to be carried, and diapers to be washed. I remember sometimes hiding in the attic for a few quiet moments to cry and catch my breath before descending again to the turmoil and demands.

I was unprepared for the warm welcome we would receive from the islanders, though I should not have been surprised. In our brief 10-day visit the year before, we were befriended and welcomed in "like family" by Collin and Kathleen Hirtle. There were few official roads on the outer islands, but there was a tacit understanding that paths could be made along the water leading from house to house.

In the first week, Simon came home from doing a carpentry errand and was stopped by one of the old fishermen, the wizened but lively Percy Baker. "I seen you was a stranger and I come out to have a yarn wit' you." Television had just come to the islands and would eventually replace the stock of stories fishermen—and women too—could spin out and linger over until they became reified as gospel.

We had landed in the middle of a small-but-vibrant fishing community contained within a cluster of islands, at the mouth of the LaHave River. Except for Malcolm Baggett, the proprietor of the only store on the island (known to all as The Shop) every able-bodied man on the islands was involved in fishing. However, fishing was changing at an accelerating rate, like everything else in the second half of the 20th century. Boats were getting engines and radar, unemployment benefits helped through the non-fishing winter months, medical expenses were absorbed by a national health scheme, and the government-sponsored support services conspicuously raised the standard of living for all Canadians. In 1968, it was all happening as post-war social programs edged into action, and more advanced technologies wiggled their way across the Canadian border.

We were privileged to arrive in the middle of change. There were too many changes happening at once to chronicle, but I can offer an example: Collin Hirtle's daughter, MaryAnne, had all her teeth removed when she was 14 to avoid later trouble. They were doing her a favor, saving her from the pain of toothaches and the financial burden of dentistry, before a national health service, before easy access to dentists. Their grandchildren would grow to maturity with a mouthful of teeth and no fear of the dentist.

Post-war social support services were making life easier for fishermen, but ironically there were fewer fish for these better supported fishing families. The fish were plentiful in 1968, but by 1980 it was clear the fish stocks were dwindling and improvements in technology could not make up the difference. Now there are a few boats in lobstering season but hardly a fish to be caught or a local market for selling the fish, should there be any. With the disappearance of fish there has been a striking decline in tidal pool life, in varieties of fish, birds, and small creatures like mink. But, even more striking, when there are no fish there are no fishing families. In a mere 100 years, the LaHave islands were settled, houses built, land cleared, and a community created. And, in half that time, the community had disappeared, the land reverting to scrubby evergreens and the houses composting themselves back into the soil.

As summer visitors "from away" in 1968, we were able to live much like the earliest settlers in our house: immigrants from Germany during the famines of the mid-19th century. We had a hand-dug well for water, an outhouse for waste, a wood stove for heat and cooking, and neighbors for help and comradeship. Some of our neighbors had animals, cows and/or chickens, or an occasional pig—and almost all had gardens with vegetables like potatoes, cabbage, and cranberries for essential vitamin C. The staple was dried salt fish. We didn't have a refrigerator, but we kept food likely to spoil in a watertight pail in the well, the coldest place available.

We were, in a sense, tourists, but also people from away living on the land or "back to nature"—a deliberate choice on our part. We left when it got cold; we had access to sophisticated medicine and dentistry. When we did abandon the 19th century life, we skipped the century between, going from no phones to a computer, from kerosene lamps to solar panels, and sailing or rowing boats to motor boats. And we were free to leave whenever we chose.

Boats? Of course. We had boats, as essential to life on the islands as wood or water. That first summer we had a new 18-foot lapstrake wooden boat with an engine in the back, which Simon bought in a local boat yard. His pride and joy, though, was an International 14, an elegant lapstrake wooden sailing boat, 14 feet long with a 25-foot mast, and a jib and a main. It went like the wind until many years later, after I made repairs with fiberglass, and it no longer could be hauled over a sand bar by two people.

We came in June, when the sun stretched out his arms as far as they would go, certainly to the ends of the known world and beyond. I would wake to the sound of the local fishing boats putt-putt-putting out Bell Channel in the silvery dawn. Most of them were single- or double-cylinder engines installed in old open, double-ended fishing boats originally designed to sail or row. A few of the more prosperous fisherman had lobster boats with a blunt stern and a small engine room up front, but these had old car engines. The specially designed marine engine appeared in boats and gradually replaced the putt-putts during our early years in Nova Scotia, but that first summer we greeted the dawn with a symphony of putt-putts.

The first morning and every morning thereafter, rain or shine, I woke to the sounds of the fishing boats and the sliver of light coming through the one attic window. Only half awake, I would roll over in bed and gather in Rebecca, who was beginning to make mumbling, fussy sounds, for a long sleepy nurse, the two us slowly waking up as she sucked and dosed. Simon slipped off his side of the mattress and reappeared 20 minutes later or so with a cup of coffee for me, freshly brewed on his old primus stove.

Simon was the first person I met who made a ritual of coffee-making, fussing over the quality of the coffee, the grind, and the brewing of it. He would buy the best coffee he could find in a fine grind and pour boiling water through the grounds "in an old sock" or the equivalent. His old sock was a small funnel-like cloth bag he had brought back from Mexico. It was very good coffee. My relatives put a spoonful of instant coffee into a cup, poured in hot water, not always "on the boil," and added canned milk. One of the many things I learned from Simon was how to be a coffee snob.

After coffee, the wild rumpus began. I struggled with the grumpy old stove to get the chill off the morning, the children fell into various patterns, some running down to the shore to check on the crabs caught the day before or to add to the assortment of shells, sea urchins, star fish, or buoys they were collecting; others stumbled into the kitchen half awake, looking for sustenance. Baby Rebecca sat nicely propped up in a cardboard box on the table, next to the salt and pepper, waving her arms in delight and giggling when tickled.

There was breakfast and bed-making and chores, such as bringing up water from the well. In later years, the red plastic buckets gained names: Bobby Bucket and Betty Bucket. Some children carried water, some wood, and Rebecca had a second milky breakfast before going back down for a nap. Then I did dishes with water heated on the wood stove and, since I hoped not to have to start it again, I usually made a soup for lunch. Simon went immediately to work on the foundations, the roof, and all the unanticipated little repairs needed to keep the house standing. Sometimes I took the children to the beach, sometimes I washed diapers and scrubbed floors, and sometimes I helped Simon on the project of the moment. I rocked Rebecca and nursed her, stopped fights, produced painting material or playing cards on rainy days, and suggested games like hide-and-seek or fort building.

Fishermen came to visit. The fishing boats which went out in near dark at 4 a.m. came back in the full glow of morning between 10 and 11 a.m. The single cylinders, the double cylinders, and the sound of a few old car engines heralded their reappearance. Between the blue of the ocean and the blue of the sky, crowds of gray, blue, and black seagulls circled around the fishing boats crying, clamoring, announcing the arrival of fish. On the way in, the fishing crews gutted and dressed their fish for selling at the "Fish Plant" on Bush Island. When the tide was high enough to get into our dock, either Collin or Nelson, both Hirtles but not from the same family, would swing up alongside the dock with "a nice mess of mackerel." I'd run up to the house for beer, Simon would settle down on the dock "for a yarn" and the children would watch wide-eyed until it got boring and then they'd go back to skimming stones, collecting shells and sand dollars, or fort building. In later years, Nelson, one of the younger fishermen, became a great favorite. He would tease them and they him, and they made a game of stealing his cap.

There were four standing houses on Middle Island in 1968, and only one was occupied year-round. Shortly after the LaHave Islands were first settled in the mid-19th century there were 10 houses on Middle Island, but only these four remained, and all were empty save one, holding a family of seven; the father, Percy Hirtle; his two daughters, Shirley and Hazel; and five surviving sons. Freddy, the youngest, was 15 that first summer and, when he wasn't fishing with one of his brothers, he would walk across the island to visit us. He didn't talk much, but he was clearly fascinated with the shingling project and would sit and watch Simon all afternoon. Freddy lived with his brothers and sisters in a two-bedroom house with an unfinished attic—probably built about a hundred years earlier—and I was told they had only one lamp between them. Percy's wife had had several babies who died before they were a year old, and she herself died of cancer shortly after the last surviving baby was born. The babies' little wood marked graves behind the house were slowly disappearing in a marsh which was itself disappearing into a pond.

The fishermen came to us and we went to them. We were as warmly welcomed by Kathleen and Collin as we had been the previous summer when we first arrived. Since there were no roads and no phones, every visit was a drop-in, but there was a wide welcome; always a cup of tea and a rocking chair. Kathleen held out her arms and I had no choice but to deposit Rebecca there. We rocked and talked. They were endlessly curious about us and we about them. We talked about our children, the winter, the weather, the price of lobster, how the mackerel harvest was doing, and local island gossip: church, politics, births and deaths—yarns.

Wonderful, well-rehearsed tales of rum running, fishing adventures, drownings, and marvels.

We packed up all that we had brought and intended to leave. The motorboat, the skiff, Sea Urchin, and the '14 were tucked away in the store. We packed the rest of our stuff into the car and went around the island to say goodbye to our new friends. "When you are comin' home again?" was always the parting question. We promised them and ourselves that we would come and when we came it would be for the whole summer. One or another of us didn't always make it for the whole summer, but as a teacher with summers off, the children and I were on the islands most of the next 50 summers, though in the last decades the number of children dwindled as they were grown up enough to have jobs, schooling, and families of their own. I replaced their energy and companionship with a coterie of friends who came every summer.

More than 50 years later, on the last day of August 2019, my granddaughter Rose and I emptied the water barrels, took down the solar panels, made sure all the perishable food was packed up to go, locked the house, the store and the boathouse—another Simon project added in the intervening years—loaded our kayaks with the last essentials and pulled off from shore. The narcissus and lilacs had gone by but small green forests of cranberry bushes clung to the rocks, suggesting fall was on the way. I looked back from the water and my eyes swept the shoreline: saying goodbye to the old, weathered house, the shingles covered with fading red paint as it had been when we arrived. I thought briefly of the paint we put on a few years after our first arrival: a paint made of fish oil, kerosene, and red ochre, a formula popular on the islands for more than a century. The old-fashioned formula was a good preservative but what a smell!

The faded red house standing alone on a small bluff was looking a little sturdier than it had 51 years earlier, but not much. As my eyes slid further down the shore, I saw the old store, several times re-shingled and blocked up, and a large new boathouse where this year's fleet of Simon-made wooden boats were shoehorned in, snug for the winter. I thought as I always did of a line from Robert McCloskeys', "Time of Wonder." The family in the book, like ours, were packing up their summer home in Maine to go back to their winter home, work, and school, feeling, "a little bit sad about the place we are leaving; a little bit glad about the place we are going."

I scanned the shore line we were leaving, reviewing the joys, setbacks and surprises of the summer and I said under my breath, "Keep safe." Then we turned our backs on Paradise and paddled toward the mainland.

July 11 White Fog evening

Fog covers Middle Island. (Courtesy of Rose Watts.)

Black T'ick a' Fog

Please, dear God, I prayed, *get me out of this safely.* The fog lay on the water, gray and palpable. Just below and a paddle length's out from the canoe, the water was a warm, flat black. Everything else was pea soup fog, damp foam rubber, something you could cut with a knife. This was what the fishermen meant when they said it was "black t'ick a' fog."

The compass between my knees—which was supposed to be showing southeast—was moving steadily with a mind of its own toward west. Which direction should one paddle in to make it swing back south? No, not that way. Well, halfway around? Could the compass possibly be right? There, all the way around again. Now to keep it steadily on south. Home was Middle Island and I knew the prevailing wind was southeast, so south would be the way to go from Bell to Middle.

It was after 8pm. Could I make the shore of Middle Island before dark? What was that low, slow sloughing? The big rock? Cabbage Head? Please God, the shore of Middle... No. A long rock. Chowder's Rock? Nothing looks the same in the fog. Wavering in the softly rolling sea, the rock was only a dark cast on an already dim place—a shadow on an under exposed negative.

When I left, paddling slowly out along the coast of Bell's Island, there were a surprising number of people down by the shore, all moving silently. Why do people become quiet when the air is quiet? A mother and daughter watched solemnly from the end of Junior's wharf, and on Percy's stage four or five dim figures moved, bringing in the gear from a day on the water.

"Some fog. Yup, some fog," a quiet greeting. Surely I could cover the short distance across Baker's Gut now, even if no sign of the opposite shore was visible. Just point the compass and stick with it.

"Aren't you afraid to be out in this fog?" A faint voice from one of the dim figures on the wharf.

"Oh, no, I've got my compass." And, to myself, I just wish I'd practiced with it in daylight and sunlight...and with this canoe. *I'm not much more experienced with a canoe than I am with a compass*, I thought ruefully.

More sloughing, getting louder now and closer, and the swells beginning to ascend and descend like heavy breathing. Something menacing loomed...mustn't get too close...a bigger rock. But what rock is this? More slight surf against a dim outline, hardly a shape but perhaps a shape in the mist, darkening. Middle Island? Doesn't look like Middle Island. Round? Sand Dollar? Cabbage. Yes, Cabbage.

Whatever it is, I'm going to land on it, I thought. Better to spend the night here than to drift out to sea. I could be lost forever. Fortunately no one is expecting me in either place so they won't be looking for me, endangering themselves. I'll just bunk down—it isn't cold—and wait until morning. Or perhaps the fog will clear a little and the moon will come out.

There, I'm sure this is the inner side of Cabbage. I'll just paddle around the point and land on the beach to be sure. From there, I might even be able to get across to Middle.

No beach. Rocks. Not a coast particularly sympathetic to landing. Hard slices of rock, then a point, perhaps unwise to get too close, but I'm not leaving this definite place for that gray blur. I'm landing. There, it's calmer on this side, and the breeze—what there is of it—is warmer, and it has a land smell. Hey, sand. Why this looks like—this is—Johnson's Point!

So, I spent three hours on Johnson's Point. I tried to make a nest in the damp sand to sleep. The bugs weren't horrible, but they weren't good. A few sand crabs. I got up to check my watch but couldn't read it. I debated whether to try again and decided not. Ran up and down the beach and hunted for a flat rock where I could do some clogging to get my feet warm. I tried burying my very wet feet in the sand to keep in the warmth they generated. Thought: *at least I'm safe. And no one's worrying about me.*

I tried reading my watch again: 10:30 pm. I can read it! Perhaps I can see those trees a few yards away a little better. Maybe the fog is clearing. I'll sleep a little more and try again. Not much sleep with the occasional mosquito but when the attack of no see'ums began, biting even through my clothes, I thought: *time to try again.* 11:45 pm. Yes, I convinced myself, without my glasses—they misted over so quickly—I can read the compass now. Home. Warm bed. Surely all I have to do is bear due east and never let it deviate. But a touch of doubt hovered; how had I managed to get so far off course?

I went due east, my compass firmly clasped between my knees again, resolutely looking only at that faint, barely discernable "E." I tried never to take my eyes off it, and to keep the sloughing on my left. Surely on this course I'll bump into Middle. Goodbye sight of Johnson's Point. Just keep dipping the paddle in the silent fog. Deep sloughing now to the right—a long, low, ominous-sounding reef. What looks like that? Mackerel Point? No. Outer Island Reef. Good grief, so far out? This is no joke. Switch the compass to north and head for in. Anywhere in.

I swung around, leaving the Outer Island Reef behind, and though I could barely make out the shadow shaped mass of land, just one shade of gray darker than the sea and the sky, close enough it seemed to touch, and yet unknowable, I paddled cautiously from point to point, never letting the shadow out of sight, and finally came to the dear, familiar coast of Middle Island. Only then did I relax enough to notice that there was phosphorescence in the water, creating sparkles with each stroke of the paddle. The sky was lightening. I saw a faint round glimmer in the haze; the moon trying to come to the rescue?

In the morning the children were surprised to see me, "Oh, we thought you were spending the night on Bell."

Nova Scotia Sunset

Mink could be seen swimming in the small pond or coming out of the woods.

Birds and Beasts on Middle Island

My family and I have been living on Middle Island as summer residents for the last 35 years. For about 25 of those years, I kept a chart of the birds I'd seen on Middle Island. It started one year fairly early in our occupancy, perhaps 1968 or '69, with an idle question from a friend in Vermont.

"What kinds of birds do you have up there?" she asked.

"Well, we have robins, and sparrows, and sea gulls, and crows, and swallows, and..."

Gosh, I thought to myself later, *those are all very common birds. I'll bet there are lots of other birds, maybe some you'd only find in a special kind of habitat like that; I'd better start looking.*

The next summer, I armed myself with a bird book and a really good pair of binoculars, and started my summer list.

I kept the list on the back of the closet door beneath the stairs on a piece of yellow card, and there it hung for years, getting older, dingier and longer. Next to it was a cartoon from a New Yorker showing a big notice board and a bird scanning it with a jaundiced eye. The notice board read, "Arrivals and Departures", with species of birds noted below. All we lacked in the closet under the stairs was the bird itself, and the jaundiced eye.

The list is too long to copy here, but suffice to say there were almost 70 birds. There undoubtedly would be more if I were anything but an amateur birder come late to the field. There were 10 seabirds, gulls, and ospreys. When there were still fish, clouds of gracefully wheeling and darting terns followed the fishing boats. The (not-so-) common loon appeared in early June and disappeared within a few weeks. Sometimes, black ducks had babies in our cove, and I watched the mamas herd their chicks into a small bunch after a big black gull dove down and snapped one up. What an uproar from the vigilant adults, stretching, splashing, rising up, and beating the water. Also in the cove: cormorants, a dime a dozen, stretching their wings out to dry, standing on the rocks or somersaulting forward into the water and shaking the silver drops off as they emerged triumphant with a fish pierced through the belly.

There were 11 types of shorebirds on the list, including plovers and sandpipers who even now rise and land on the beach in choreographed crowds. I counted 15 varieties of warblers—easier to hear than see, as they seem never to stay still for a minute, whether overhead or under the camouflage of leaves on a branch. Eight varieties of the ubiquitous sparrow: my favorite is the song sparrow who nests close to the house and sings his way through June, winding up with three toots followed by something like a crescendo of muted piano keys. In with sparrows are finches in three colors: red, purple, and gold. I also saw a murder of crows traveling at dawn and dusk between their roosting trees and the open skies, creatures of legend in many cultures. Percy Baker, friend and fisherman, told Simon: "One crow is bad luck, but two crows is good luck."

Finally, the familiar birds: cardinals, red-winged black birds, arboreal chickadees, swallows, cat birds, cowbirds, and, of course, robins. Some of our familiar birds appear in Canadian colors: boreal chickadees have brown where American chickadees are black, and the Canada Jay is as loud and raucous as the Blue Jay but with muted feathering.

Almost all of these birds really have been seen or heard on Middle Island over the last 30 years, though I cheated on a few, particularly the sea birds, adding them from sightings at Crescent Beach, Bay Beach, Creek Beach, Outer Island, and Bell's Island. I've listed the birds roughly in the order they appear in my ragged, loose paged, much thumbed, often damp and curling "Peterson's Guide."

Recently, I have noticed a significant decline in the number of birds altogether. When we first came to the islands the sky above our cove was often alive with terns, especially in the early morning. I watched them soaring, gliding, and then plunging in at what one would think must be neck breaking speed, bill down, piercing the water, and then up, usually with a small fish flapping helplessly in the bill. The cries of the gliding, hunting terns filled the air. Some of these terns nested on Thrum Cap; once I almost stepped on a nest concealed in the grass and never dared to return in the nesting season.

Now, at the beginning of the 21st century, there are only a few terns, and they do not nest on Thrum Cap. Modern improvements in technology and an increasing number of large trawlers from many nations scraping the ocean floor, often with rakes four miles long, destroyed the habitat for fish and other sea creatures. When the fish go, the creatures which live on the fish must also go. I grieve for the absence of those slim-winged, swift diving, beautifully adapted creatures and for the off-shore fishing communities which disappeared for the same reasons.

For a few years in the '70s, we were inundated with barn swallows. They built nests in the store, in the outhouse, and wherever else they could find a ledge and shelter. The ones in the outhouse (nicknamed "the birdie house" by one summer's worth of children) were wont to dive bomb us when we went in and out as much as to say, "who's house is this, anyway?" There are still five or six bird houses placed advantageously on out buildings to encourage compatible housing arrangements. In the evening, the swallows dipped back and forth between the outbuildings, in hot pursuit of insects, their weaving and dipping a delight to observe. One year, at the peak of the nesting season, we had two days of very high winds. The swallows disappeared, presumably holed up in the woods to escape the savagery of the wind, but few of the eggs or young survived. We have never had a richness of swallows since; indeed, many years there are no swallows at all.

We raised a baby sea gull one summer when my son Richard was about ten. We'd taken a sea trip to Indian Island, where the trees have been killed by cormorant colonies nesting off the ground and sea gulls by the thousands nesting along the shore. Indian Island has a rockbound coast; landing is difficult, but flying in is no problem for the gulls and cormorants. We pulled a small boat off from the double ender and someone stood by it on the surfy pebble beach while we did a quick scouting, deafened by the cries of outrage from the gulls disturbed and swarming. We didn't stay long and, when we got back to the big boat, I discovered that Richard and his friend Michael had taken a baby bird from one of the nests, newly hatched with a bit of shell on the wing.

I had just read Tinbergen's book on sea gull behavior, so I was determined that we should raise the gull in a way that would save it from becoming dependent on us. The boys built an outside pen for Queep-Queep, as they called him—a fair rendition of the way he talked—and then set about finding food. They came to me in alarm. He wasn't eating anything. When I told them that baby sea gulls are fed on the raw fish their parents catch, partly chewed and regurgitated, Michael valiantly tried chewing the raw fish and spitting it out in a maneuver worthy of Farley Mowat himself. In *Never Cry Wolf*, Mowat describes how he lived for months on a diet of mice to show that wolves could do the same. In spite of these tender preparations, Queep-Queep stood on one foot or another queeping pitifully but not eating the fish so carefully placed before him. Then I remembered Tinbergen's description of the young gull pecking at a red spot on the adult's beak to release the food. We realized that if the food were held above him, rather than on the ground, old man instinct would show him how to get it. It worked, and gradually the boys taught him how to eat from a dish on the ground but that was the only thing we ever taught that bird. He ate and strutted around until his feathers came in, and then we took him down to the water. He needed a little encouraging to go in, but in he went, returning after each swim to where we were standing.

There were other gulls in the cove of course and, like any other young gull, Queep-Queep began following around one adult or another, doing his "poor starving me, queep queep" routine until, in exasperation, one or another of the adult gulls would feed him. Eventually, he learned to fly and by the end of the summer was quite independent, though he returned almost every night to sleep on the ridge pole above his pen. Before we left for the summer, he had disappeared into the anonymous mass of gulls in the cove, but the following summer a gull would often perch on the ridge of the roof and I liked to think that it was Queep-Queep come back to check on us.

The wildlife on Middle Island is not limited to things with wings. Almost every summer, there are deer; you can see the sharp indentations of their hoofs on the beaches, so fresh you know you have just missed them, and know also that they may be peering cautiously at you that very moment from the woods. Another sure sign of deer is the nibbled lilies, down sometimes to the nub, which used to welcome us in the spring. Occasionally, we catch a glimpse of them—usually a mother and fawn— and frightened visitors tell stories about being surprised by loud snorting, sniffing, and sometimes even barking along the wood's line. For many years, but not recently, I'd come back to find a fresh blind on the edge of the pond, constructed, I assumed, by a fisherman waiting for duck or deer during hunting season. I like to think that the hunters were kids once on Middle Island, coming back to hunt for meat as their fathers must have done before them.

Deer are the largest animals on Middle Island; the smallest you can see are the moles and voles, in the hundreds and the thousands, I suspect. Certainly, there seems to be a small army which comes out at night to nibble on my marigolds and lettuce, and any time of day or night you may catch a glimpse of a little gray creature high tailing it between clumps of matted grass. One summer, when our girls were small, they and their neighboring friends, Amy and Jenny Rees captured some voles that Amy carried around in a nest of straw inside an old teakettle. When the cats caught a vole, they were inclined to nibble the head and a few other parts, then leave the mutilated carcass on our back doorstep. The big girls considered this yucky and developed a strategy to solve the problem by persuading the younger girls to remove them to prove they were not squeamish. One day, sitting on a bench by the back door in the sun, I heard one little girl announce to the other: "I'm not screamish. Are you?" "NO" came the decisive answer, and then, "What's screamish?"

In between the big deer and the little voles, we have seen mink, muskrat, sea otters, and beaver. Yes, really. I used to go to the fresh water pond to watch the muskrat diving and playing at dawn or twilight, and one famous summer one of the creatures sporting in the water sighted me and womped the water with her tail. I was incredulous. How could beavers get out here? Perhaps I was mistaken. But I continued to watch them, and they continued to behave more like beavers than like muskrats. That same summer, we were playing around with the canoe on the pond, and once, when my sister and I were in the canoe together, we paddled past a thick clump of bulrushes and saw a large brown animal cowering inside. I reached in and my hand encountered something tail-like broad, flat and rubbery. That was no muskrat! I assume the beavers came over on the ice in the winter and swam away later in the summer.

Two or three different summers we saw a fox, sometimes red, sometimes gray. We saw the mink occasionally but not often, streaking between rocks or swimming to shore. "There goes a nice pair of gloves," said one of the local women when we stood together watching one swimming around the rocks. The mink, like the deer, can become pests. One summer, when I came up early, there was a family of mink living under the house. I could catch a glimpse of the adults streaking between the cellar and the shore, using the big pine tree for cover on the way, and I could hear the babies squeaking out, "That must have been a mighty fine town-o, town-o," when the parents returned with supper. But the smell! And the mess!

Sea otters I saw once, sporting around the rocks off Magic beach. They were doing what the book says they do: swimming on their backs in the water with clam shells clutched to the chest. The slim five fingered paw marks of the sea otters are sometimes overlaid with the smaller hand or footprint of a raccoon—or several. If there are other wild creatures on Middle Island I have yet to meet them, but the possibility adds incentive to move quietly and look closely.

Tides can drop six feet on a full moon. (Courtesy Rose Watts.)

The Tide and I

In, out, up, back, advance, retreat
Immutable, inexorable, indefatigable
The tide and I play tag.

Puff balls of spun spray skitter down the beach.
Dissolve in mid-air
Come to rest in the wrack of the tide line.

I stop to look: a silvery filigree of tiny bubbles
Rainbows in the big ones
Nesting in wind tossed, homeless eelgrass.

Behind me, footprints fill with icy water,
The bossy wind shoves and pushes
Suddenly one sneaker is cold and wet
Tagged by the tide.

I hear voices but see no people.
To the north the line drawn by tide on sand
Shrinks to an uninterrupted point in blue haze.
To the east the white horses toss their manes
(Impossible to resist that ancient imagery).
To the west, a towering wall of sandy cliff
Denies the advancing calvary.

And to the south,
Only the blustering beautiful sea
Overhead, Oh! Two geese just checkin' in,

Some Wonderful

Dark silhouettes in the bright morning sun.
I shield my eyes from the light
Watching the exuberance of the waves and
The spurts of surf high-fiving.

In, out, up, down, advance, retreat
Immutable, irrestible, indefatigable.
The tide and I play tag.

July 12 Crescent Beach Seaweed

Inside the front door is a long counter and shelves filled with canned milk and peas. (Courtesy Heidi Watts.)

FISHERMEN STORIES

The Shop on Bell's Island

Is it open? I asked myself, glancing at once, from habit, to see whether the small iron bar of the latch extended over the crack between door and frame. Open, I decided, since no interruption in the space was visible. Other shops with which I was familiar advertise their willingness to take your money loudly, with signs, flashing lights, or at least an "Open" sign. Not the shop on Bell's Island.

Only if the 2 inches of iron bar was drawn to the left rather than the right could you be sure, in spite of the dark window and the silence encasing the shop like smoke, that there would be someone inside. Although the proprietor's house was less than thirty feet from this center of commerce, on this isolated island of approximately ten families, the shop was never left unlocked. If the door was unbarred, either Malcolm or Jessie would be inside.

Today, it was Malcolm—Mr. Baggett—leaning back in his straight chair behind the counter to catch what light came through the single window, reading an adventure novel he had taken from the Book Mobile's most recent deposit. There was a light bulb over his head, the string hanging down to hand—but why waste electricity if you can make out the print without it?

"Hullo", he said, as I creaked open the inner door and pushed through the screen door, "Hullo, Haldie, warm enough for you?"

"Yes," I said, sinking down gratefully on the gray bench in front of the counter. "It's wonderful to have it warm at last."

"You sail in?" he asked, standing up slowly to signal his readiness to do business, and I responded on cue, "Let's see, I need eggs, and butter, and bacon, oh, and canned milk." Although the butter would come out of a refrigerator and the bacon from the freezer, Malcolm never carried fresh milk. Before electricity came to the islands the fishermen relied upon canned milk, and, although they'd had electricity for 40 years, refrigerators for 30, and a road to the mainland for four, the shop continued to stock what it had always stocked.

As Malcolm lumbered slowly towards the back room to count out twelve eggs from the big crate I looked carefully around the shop, fixing the landscape in my mind. Canned milk filled two shelves, one shelf for Carnation, one for Pet. This in itself was a concession: baked beans in cans were the only other commodity offered in more than one brand. Over the top shelf, which ran the length of the shop on the left, cans of pamplemousse, French side out, and cans of tomato juice marched side by side. The shelves below displayed chewing and pipe tobacco, matches, tea, and canned fruits and vegetables. Prices were indicated on small bits of neatly cut cardboard, thumbtacked to each shelf and lettered in pencil. They looked as though they had been there since World War II.

Similar shelves, stocked with crackers, candy or corned beef, Spam, and boxes of soap lined all the available wall space on the other side. On the right side also, a wide gray bench ran before the counter for the convenience of fishermen who came to the shop as much to chat as to buy. All of the woodwork, except for the facing benches, was painted with a high-gloss, pale green enamel, now dulled by time and the fumes from the kerosene stove at the end of the small room.

I put my feet up on the bench and leaned back against the front wall; this was going to be a social as well as a business call. As my eyes adjusted to the light, I could just make out the soda case in the far corner: plain, gray, waist high. Inside, the bottles of grape and orange soda would be lined up like perspiring soldiers, small drops of moisture clinging to the sides, and, when you lifted the lid, a welcome wave of cool air would escape into the room like a genie let out of a bottle. When the children were younger, it had been the main attraction of the shop. Bribed by the promise of a bottle of purple pop or Orange Crush they could always be induced to row over to the shop for the tea or the matches which were needed immediately.

Malcolm came back to his place at the counter and carefully tied a string around the eggs in their paper bag. *Dear God*, I thought, as I had so often thought before, *eggs in a paper bag, help me to get them home intact in that tippy boat.*

"What have you got for fresh vegetables," I asked, knowing the answer already.

"Potatoes," he said, looking at me solemnly, "and onions and carrots."

"No cabbage?"

"No cabbage." And certainly no lettuce or celery, or any other vegetable which would have been unavailable thirty years ago, though I knew Malcolm went to town twice a week by car now. Every year, there were fewer fishermen in the shop and more summer residents like us but, although tastes and needs changed, the stock remained the same, back there in time.

While I watched, he wrapped the butter too. The edge of brown paper gave a sharp, gratifying "grrr" as he ripped it off the paper cutter, and then reached up automatically for the thin end of string which ran from a spool above, through three galvanized eyes, and down to hand's reach just above the counter. I loved the old string and paper routine, and I loved the old weighing machine with its pinched-in waist and white enamel frame, standing smugly on the counter between the candy bars and a small box of fresh plums: the luxury item for the week at 15 cents a plum.

"Now, what else do I need?" I mentally ticked off the staples: sugar, yeast, toilet paper, rosebuds—ah, rosebuds! Small candy kisses, innocent of silver paper. The delight of the young, and of the old too for that matter. Under a glass cover, just over there behind the candy bars, loose in three compartments sat the mints, macaroons, and rosebuds. For seventy-five cents a pound of the latter, carefully weighed on the enamel scale and wrapped in brown paper, could go home to be measured out again, "How many each, Mummy?"

"One, two, three, four, five, six, seven, eight, nine, ten—ten for you Rebecca. "One, two...ten for Elianne. Ten for me." No need to make dessert tonight; another hour from the kitchen cheaply purchased.

"Malcolm, who reads those books?" I asked, pointing to a small collection on the opposite counter, half-hidden behind the Tip-Top bread and sweet rolls. They were mostly paperbacks of the romantic or swashbuckling variety, a few of the currently popular catastrophe type, a hard cover book on fish cookery, though the shop never stocked fish—that would be like selling potatoes in Aroostock County—and the ubiquitous set of Reader's Digest Condensed Books.

"Why," he said cautiously, "I read most of them. Jerry reads some, and then there's the two kids over on Wolfe's Island." It was a nice idea, bringing a fresh supply of books from the Book Mobile once a month, and underscored the fact that the shop was, in all its unadorned simplicity, the only public meeting place on the islands now. Here, I remembered, a fisheries announcement on what to do with banded salmon had appeared on one of the supporting posts last summer. Other public notices would go here—where else?

"Oh, and Malcolm, could I use your phone?" It wasn't a public phone—indeed, it was their only phone and it was here in the shop, not up in the house. However, getting to a telephone anywhere on the islands was an adventure in itself, and it would be a cold day in Hell, I thought to myself, before we'd want a telephone on Middle Island.

"You could use it," he said ponderously, leaning on his hands and blinking owlishly, "but you can't use it because it's out of order."

The door behind me scraped and the bell tinkled as Jessie momentarily blocked the entrance. She was wearing one of her flowered polyester dresses, carefully covered with a very clean, white apron, and her round face was wreathed in permanent curls. She had heard the last of her husband's words and her plucked eyebrows rose in astonishment at such a bold-faced lie. She giggled and he gazed back at her impassively.

"It's out?" I said, "For how long?" And then, "How are you, Jessie?"

"Not too bad, Haw-di", she said. "Ain't it a fine day?" And to Malcolm, "I'm making a cake for the variety supper and I just come down to get some lemon extract."

Malcolm reached down and grabbed the extract and, making a note of it on a small pad, explained, "They're workin' on it now." Then Jessie, smiling and nodding, disappeared up the hill and the door creaked shut again.

Might as well wait, I thought, though I didn't have much hope. The children were at their cousins and would be in no hurry to get home. "Malcolm, do you know that story Vernon Baker tells about John Berrigan and the lemon extract? I just heard it from him last night."

"Nope," he said, in a neutral tone and I proceeded to retell the story while Malcolm listened impassively. I'd taken a small jar of Middle Island jam to Joyce and Vernon, an excuse to stop in, and Vernon, who was born on Middle Island, began telling stories about John Berrigan, the last owner but one of the house we lived in now.

I'd knocked on the kitchen door, knowing enough to abjure the formal front door, which was never used, and Vernon had invited me in for a cup of coffee. After we'd commiserated a while over the unreliable state of the weather and the havoc of winter storms, I asked him whether he'd known John Berrigan. He was leaning with his elbows on the table and now, with a grin and a sideways, deprecating shake of his head, he said, "Ayuh, John Berrigan he was somethin'. He had this little pipe, yew," sketching a small pipe out of the side of his mouth, "and he really loved his rum." I remembered the dusty green bottles we'd found hidden in the crawl space below the house, bottles with berries fermented in the bottom. "But when he couldn't get his rum," Vernon went on, "why, he'd drink lemon juice."

"Straight lemon juice?" I heard the astonishment in my voice.

"Ayuh. He had one of them big sails, and he'd put it on his little punt, and he could sail that thing good, yew, as good as most people can sail a yacht. And he'd sail over to the shop on Bell's Island, over there," waving in the general direction of their kitchen door, "and he'd go in, and the fellas would be sitting around talkin', you know, but he wouldn't stay that long."

Malcolm was still deadpan. "I suppose that was before you owned the shop, Malcolm?" I asked.

Malcolm nodded, "Ayuh, that'd have been Jim Tumblin's shop." But he said no more so I continued.

"'So then,' Vernon had said, 'John Berrigan'd set there for a little while, yew, and then he'd say, "Well, Hattie's bakin' a cake, so I guess I'd better take some of that lemon flavorin,'" and the shopkeeper would give him a bottle of lemon extract. So then, pretty soon, he'd go down to the boat and you could see him take the bottle out of his pocket, pull out the cork and just drink it down." Here Vernon threw back his head and raised his hand to show how the bottle of lemon extract was emptied down his throat.

"Ayuh," Vernon had continued, "so then he'd set the sail and come over to Corkum's shop, down here," with a wave in the direction of the wall opposite the kitchen door, "and he'd go in and he'd say, 'Hattie's bakin' a cake so I need some of that lemon flavorin', and soon as he'd got back to the boat, down it'd go.' Here he made the appropriate motions again, emphazing the final swallow. And of course they all knew what he was doin."

He'd grinned, and Malcolm, I saw, was grinning too.

"Oh," I'd said, finally getting it, "there's alcohol in those extracts?"

"Ayuh, it'd give you quite a kick I imagine. Quite a kick."

Malcolm looked less dour as I concluded the story with a sideways shake of the head, like Vernon's, and for a moment I thought I might be rewarded by one of his stories. Malcolm could tell some good ones too, but the bell jangled and young David Hirtle lumbered in, greeting me with "Hul-lo, Mrs. Wa-atts", and handed Malcolm a list from his mother, so I gathered up my eggs and rosebuds, decided the telephone call wasn't that important after all, and said goodbye, aware that I was leaving with more than my money's worth.

Percy Baker, 1893–1992. (Courtesy Mary Bloom.)
"I won't be leaving much behind. I'm going to enjoy it while I'm here."

The Slacker

I stood on the deck and raised my hand to shade my eyes from the glare of the sun, low in the sky now, but leaving it slowly these long June days.

"Rebecca," I said, to the long-legged 11 year old beside me, "who do you think that could be?" There was no reply. Rebecca was lying on her belly, her head hung over the edge of the dock, absorbed in the antics of a rock crab, wavering in and out of the brown and yellow weed below the pilings.

The bright yellow, double-ended dory came efficiently through the shimmery haze on the water, the oars dipping cleanly with the long pull of an experienced fisherman. It might be David Hirtle, but the dark back was too slight. . . .. It might be. . . . "Oh, it's Percy Baker." The boat was close enough now to reveal the silhouette of a small thin man bending to the oars. I was glad Rebecca was there. The summer folk called him "Pinchin' Percy," and he himself, 85 but still spry and still fishing, said, "I ain't done with the women yet."

He had come over, the second summer I'd been up to the islands after my husband left me, with a bottle of whiskey and some fresh mackerel, "courtin'!" The recollection of it made me smile again, now, as I remembered the little man, not more than a hundred pounds of him, I'd guess, his sharp eyes and foxy face at about the level of my chin, "A good lookin' woman like you, Haldie, you oughter have a man."

"No, Percy," I'd said, amused and surprised, "I don't think I want anyone else right now."

"Well, Percy," I said, hooking the painter around the post for him, "How nice to see you."

"Fine night, Haldie", he said, clambering up the ladder. "I brought you some corn herrin'. You ever eat corned herrin'?"

"No, I never did."

"Wal, now, you just cook 'em up wit' a little water and eat 'em wit' new potaters. Brought you' some potaters too. They're right nice."

He set the pail down, carefully, and I could see the silver scales reflecting on the irridescent skin. "Lovely weather we been havin', but it wants showers for tomorra." And then, peering blindly at Rebecca, "Who's this now?"

"This is Rebecca," I said, with that quick flash of pride I felt at the mention of any of my children. "The others are coming later."

He turned his head toward me, one ear raised as though to catch the sound better, and said, "Beg pardon?"

He's getting really deaf, I thought, and raised my voice to a shout. "This is Rebecca. Did you have a good winter?" Rebecca turned her head for a momentary smile of acknowledgement and then went back to crab antics.

"Oh, not too bad, not too bad."

"Come up and sit awhile. Would you like a beer?"

He grinned at me. "A little, if it ain't no trouble. I just come out to have a yarn wit' you. You don't need a' be afraid of me, Haldie. I just come out for a yarn."

I dispatched Rebecca for two bottles of beer and an opener, and led the way up the grassy embankment to the deck on the front of the house. The mosquitos weren't too bad at this time of year, and sitting there we could watch the sun set behind the old Berrigan house across the cove. I sat on the edge with my bare feet buried in the long grass, and wondered idly how we were going to get it cut this year. He settled close beside me—only to hear better, I hoped. The sky was rosy now, making the pointed firs on the Berrrigan land nearly black. If the scale were different, they might well be ferns whose lacy indentations against the deepening dusk created a border between earth and air.

"So, Percy, what's new?"

"Nawthin' much, Haldie. Had a real bad storm this spring. Took out my whole wharf, yew. Me and Wergil had to go over to the Cape and get all new poles for her. You never saw the water so high."

Why was it the old generation on the islands always put a "w" where a "y" should be and never said the "th?" Was it something left from their German origins? A dialect that refined and perpetuated itself?

Percy was telling me how to cook the herring. "Just a little water in the bottom of the pan. You can put in a few onions if you like, an' you simmer 'em up, and then you' eat 'em wit' new potaters and they're some good."

As I thanked him I watched the sun slipping down, half of that gorgeous orange plate already gone behind the trees—that's right, it wouldn't set behind the old house until much later in the summer I reminded myself—

and then I remembered what I really wanted to ask him. "Were you ever in the army, Percy?"

"Wal, now," he grinned at me, "I wasn't never. I was one of them fellers they call slackers."

"Was that the first war or the second?"

"The first. It ain't that I was afraid, my good woman", and he put his hand on my knee—for emphasis perhaps? I let it stay; what harm could it do?

"I was out in the boats, in all weathers, in the winter, way up to the banks, yew, I was shipwrecked..."

"Yes, I know," I interrupted quickly, "that's a wonderful story, but tell me about the slackers."

My husband? ...Absent husband?... Soon to be ex husband? had already recorded that story in what had once been a joint endeavor to capture and cherish the fisherman's yarns.

"Ayuh", switching gears smoothly, "We was out to Wancouver for the halibut harvest." He straightened and shifted, as if setting his back to the pleasant task of yarning through these familiar waters. "We was out to Wancouver, me an' my mate, for the harvest. The halibut harvest. Ye see, they was takin' the fellers about two months earlier out there then back here. Wal, one day this feller comes up to me, and he puts his hand on my shoulder, see..."

He turned sightly to indicate the weight of a hand on his shoulder, "an' he says 'We gotta go for the army.' He wants to see our papers and everyt'in'. So we went down to the boat and got 'em, an' he says we gotta' sign up. Then I says, 'Where you gonna' send us to drill?' An' he says, 'Dunno, maybe to China.'"

We both chuckled at the joke. "Then I says, 'cain't you send us back home, 'round Halifax, to drill?' an' he says, 'Wal, I'll tell you in the mornin.'"

"In the morning he says 'Wal, we can go back home,' and when we get there they'll tell us what to do. So we went back to Halifax, two nights on the train, an' we got in early in the mornin'. I didn't see nobody to tell me what to do," he winked slyly, "so I went for home. Then all summer I was out wit' the boats, and come fall, I quick skipped on a boat down to the Grand Banks." One hand sliced across the other and through the air to indicate the swiftness of that skip. "I *never* spent too much time to home."

"Then it was all over, you know, but they was after some of us fellers, 'slackers' they called us, to pay a fine." He shook his head. "But when they come out to the islands, I wasn't never to home. They'd come in one door and I'd be out the other." He winked again, including me in the conspiracy.

"One day, I was to Bridgewater wit' my father and I see'd this feller comin' down the street, a secret service man, yew. So I leans back," putting the words to action, "an' he has this picture of me in his hand." He cupped his hand and held it at arm's length to peer at it, "an' he says to me, 'You ever hear of a feller called Percy Baker?'"

"An' I says, I t'ink I heared that name afore."

"'Well,' he says, 'we're lookin' for him, but every time we go down to the islands he ain't there. They say he's up to Bridgewater, but up here in Bridgewater they say he's down to the islands. You t'ink he's home now?'"

"'I dunno,' I says, 'you could try. I t'ink I heared of him down there.' They didn't recognize me, yew, 'cause I had on city clothes then. I looked some swell when I was dressed up in those days. I had these fancy pants. . ." His hands indicated the sharp crease and the fancy shirt. "Oh," He shook his head, "I was some swell lookin' feller in those days."

"When I got home, my mother says, 'They was out here lookin' for you again, and they're gonna get you sooner or later. They lef' a note sayin' you hafta be to Lunenburg, to the Silver Hotel, Room 12, tomorrer mornin' ten o'clock. You better go and get it over wit,' she says."

"So the next mornin' I put a t'ousand dollars in my pocket, and I up to Riverport, and took a taxi to Lunenburg. Then, ten o'clock, Silver Hotel, Room 12." He knocks firmly on the dock, "The door opens and the officer says, 'Who're you?'"

"'I'm the feller you bin lookin' for and cain't find,' I says."

"He stands back, an' he looks at me an' he says, 'Was you to Bridgewater yestiddy?'"

"'Ayuh,' I says, 'but you didn't know me then.'"

"'Wal, you're here now,' he says, 'and you'll have to go to Halifax wit' us tomorrer and you'll have to stand your suit.'"

"We goes to Halifax the next day and the secretary she wants to know all about me, an' these two officers lay a' halt of me, like they're gonna lock me up, yew."

"Then the secret service men say, 'Oh, he's O.K. He's gonna pay his fine and all. We'll take care a' him tonight.'"

"They're stayin' at a boardin' house, yew, so they say, 'Look, you come along wit' us, and we'll say you're a new man on the job, helpin' to pick up slackers along the shore, an' you can sleep wit' us tonight.'"

"We goes to the boardin' house, and there are these two women there. One plays the pianner real nice, an' the other sings, an' I t'inks, I'll get one a dem to go out wit' me. So I asks the pianer lady to show me a bit of the town. 'I'm new here, I sez, Just breakin' in, an' I'd like to see a bit a' the town.'"

"'Wal, there couldn't be a safer man to go out wit,' she says, an' so we go to town, an' I'm playin' green. So green." He shook his head and grinned disarmingly, "She's showin' me this, an' pointin' out that, an' I'm pretendin' I *never* saw none a' it afore in my life. We comes in around 'leven o'clock, an' I goes up wit' the other two to sleep."

"'I hope you'll look me up if you ever come to town again,' she says, but I never did."

"The next day, the judge wants to know alt about the boats i been on an' every little t'ing. I was shipwrecked, I says an' I lost all my papers." He made the motions of turning out a set of empty pockets.

"'Wal, if you' won't tell us, we knowed anyways,' he says, real mad, and they opened up a big book, an' there's everyt'ing, all the ships, the cargo, an' the capt'ins and everyt'ing. 'So,' he says, 'we see you got two brothers was fightin' an' one stayed over there an' dat's lucky for you. Your fine should be a t'ousand dollars, but since they was in the fightin' it'll only be seven hunnerd.'"

"Seven hunnerd dollars, that's more n' enough, I says, an' then he gets some mad." Again, the quick flash of his grin beamed out to me.

"After I paid my fine we went into this other room, wit' these two cops. One a them reaches into a drawer an' pulls out two rewolvers. 'What's them for?' I says."

"'We're goin' out to the shore for them other slackers, an' you knowed 'em all, so you can tell us where they are.'"

"'Oh, no, I ain't gonna blow on them,' I says, and then to me, 'cause one a' them would a' shot me for sure."

"'But,' I says, 'I'll tell you where one feller is, down to Dublin Shore, if you'll give me a ride down there. So, they gives me a ride, an' all the way home, goin' along the shore, they're shootin' crows out of the trees wit' them rewolvers. We comes to this house where Rupert Baker lives, yew. I seed him down there, in his white shirt, rockin' in front of the winder, an' I knowed he wasn't no slacker so they couldn't *pin* it onto him so I says, 'there's your man,' an' then I hops out the back an...'" again, he made a swift slice through the air, one hand across the other, and winked at me.

The sun was well gone now, leaving jet streaks of gold in the low clouds behind the dark, fir-jagged edge of Berrrigan's Point. Rebecca had disappeared somewhere, probably back into *Anne of Green Gables*.

"Oh, Percy," I said, laughing, "that's a wonderful story."

"Ayuh," he said, "I was a wild one once, but I never done nuthin' real bad. An' now I ain't so wild but I enjoy everythin'. The flowers on the bushes, an' the nice days, an' the color in the water, an' everythin'. Probably never stopped to notice 'em afore, yew." He stood up. "Wal, Haldie, I gotta go afore it gets dark. You ain't lonesome out here, all by yourself, a good-lookin' woman like you?"

I wondered how he could tell. "No, I'm not lonesome." And indeed I wasn't. There was, as he said, so much to notice. The birds, for instance, as a cloud of black crows, their wings stirring the air with a soft hushing sound flew eastward over the cove, the way they did every night, going "home" to roost. They'd be back in the morning, as regular as commuting office workers. He interrupted my thoughts again, rising slowly to leave. "Your husband now, he got hisself another woman back there to home, I bet."

Yes, he has, I thought ruefully, with a wave of the old pain, "Yes, I suppose he has."

"Wal, now, you're free then."

"Yes, Percy," I said, smiling down at him, "Yes, I'm free now." Pushing down a flood of questions and emotions; whatever did "free" mean? "Yes, I'm free now." He was still watching me. "But I don't want anyone else right now."

"Wal, it's gettin' dark. No offense?"

"No offense," I said, laughing, as we walked toward the dock. "Thanks for the herring." I handed him the painter. "And come again sometime."

"Wal, you're a good woman, Haldie," he said, peering up at me from the dory. "If you ever get lonesome, come in an' I'll give you a glass of whiskey."

Fishermen Stories

July 15 Fresh Mussels for Dinner

The Black Hirtles

We called them the Black Hirtles, but there was nothing black about them. When there are five or six families with the same surname on a cluster of lightly populated islands you need some means of distinguishing one from the other. The Black Hirtles, like those other Hirtles, were three generations down from the first Hirtles who fled from the famines in Germany to these islands at the mouth of the LaHave River in Canada. When we arrived on the LaHave islands in the mid-1960s Percy Hirtle's family: five sons, two daughters and the old man, were living in a small cottage in poor condition on Middle Island. Where there had once been ten houses on the Island, there were only three left standing, and theirs the only one occupied. There was no electric power on Middle Island, then or now, no plumbing, no roads, no commerce.

Percy Baker and his wife had thirteen children but by the time we arrived on the islands there were only eight Hirtles left: the old man, his five grown sons and two daughters. The remaining five children died in childbirth or shortly thereafter. Shirley performed all the women's jobs: cooking, cleaning, washing. Hazel helped but was disabled from birth, and the men fished. The old man and most of the other men had their own fishing boats and as the conditions for fishing improved they became more prosperous: most of them bought new fishing boats. But that was later.

I was told, and I am sure it is true, they had only one kerosene lamp in the small house on Middle Island: one kerosene light for eight people! I doubt there were flashlights, but perhaps the lamp could be carried from place to place. On moonless nights when the fishing sons came up from the dock at night their feet would have had to feel the way; knowing where that particular stumble-causing rock lay on the path, knowing to make a half turn towards the house, slightly to the left, before the side door. And not just the feet; taking cues from the sea smells receding, the direction of the wind on the face, familiar sounds of voices, a pot put down definitively, the smell of supper, the upper step on the porch that creaked, that particular one at the top which creaked in protest, and inside, feeling the door knob, responding to a voice from the dark interior: "That you, Nelson? Boats OK?"

And not just the feet—all the senses responding to familiar smells—perhaps coffee or fried fish; to the feel of other presences; to low murmurs, coughs, a familiar groan from a person or another creak from a tired board on the stairs, without sight the other senses come into play.

The following summer when we arrived we discovered the last house occupied on Middle Island was deserted. The Hirtles experienced a totally unexpected windfall in the form of an American doctor who offered them $500.00 and a bottle of rum for their house. The doctor had been buying deserted houses for taxes, slowly building a good investment for his retirement. The Hirtles immediately bought a larger house on the next island which had electricity and a road to the mainland ($500.00 could go a long way on the islands at that time). The new house was two stories, with a big dock in good condition—and neighbors! The first thing they did was to paint the new house a shiny black and then hang it with Christmas lights: because they could.

Five Simon Watts crafted boats pointing west off the dock as the tide drops and the wind rises. "Goin' to blow somethin' awful."

Bound to Happen

"What was it like? Your first time in an airplane?" they asked Ernest Baker, fisherman for sixty years. He thought a moment, smiled and replied, "Like goin' out to the salmon nets on a fine morning in June."

It was a fine morning in June, when David Hirtle drowned. The sea was calm and a deep cerulean blue. Sun streaks danced on barely rippled water. Standing by the dock, waiting for the little girls to gather all the possessions they seemed to feel they needed for a trip to Bell Island, I could hear trills, chips, whistles, the song of one bird overlaid on another. In the fir, there beside the house a song sparrow, reving up with three short toots and then an extended trill; here in the small tree by the dock a yellow warbler singing his heart out "witchety, witchety, whee." Somewhere nearby but not in the same tree a Yellow Throat and from behind the house "Poor Sam Peabody, Peabody, Peabody. . ."

It reminded me of the children's chant: "Evangeline, Evangeline, the fattest woman you've ever seen!" And so she was. As wide as she was high, covered by a shapeless faded flower print cotton, often with an apron and an old elbowed through cardigan of her husband's. Her stockings, rolled below the knee, covered legs like those on an old oak table. We caught a glimpse of her occasionally as she clambered heavily out of a boat at the mailboxes, and she'd stop for a brief chat: "How are you? Ain't the weather some fine (or some bad?) When'cha get here?" But nothing more.

"Hurry up!" I called to the girls, and let my eyes run lovingly around the shoreline of the cove, noting again the changes on the beach the winter storms had made, and then traveling the length of the point, a snout of land reaching into the water and blocking off the view of Bell Island, where we were headed. Beyond the point, a small collection of rocks and islands scrunched in the water, and beyond them the long thin line of rock and trees which represented the mainland. No other houses in sight, and only one light at night. Once they sailed round the point, they'd see plenty of houses, fishermen's cottages mostly, with fish stores, sheds and docks. The other islands, nearer into the mainland were more populated now.

Ah, the two girls were coming at last, clutching jackets, books, and trolls. I got them all into the boat, lifted the sails, delegated one to untie from the mooring and the other to fend off, and within minutes we were drifting slowly out of the cove.

Just enough wind—barely enough—filled the sail on the port tack and the boat moved off through the water with a gentle lap-lapping sound, chuckling with pleasure at its own motion. I felt like chuckling myself: the first fine day since we'd arrived for the summer, and that was nearly a week ago. The sea and the air seemed released from care, as I was released finally from running back and forth between the wood pile and the stove.

Rebecca and her bosom friend, Elianna, seemed hardly aware they were in a boat. Bosum friend, hmm. . . . I'd been reading *Anne of Green Gables* aloud to the girls this summer, and found myself thinking in that language sometimes. The girls chattered away about plans for a troll wedding and about what they would buy at the shop when I dropped them off.

If I looked up, I could see the great white wing of the sail, and the top of the mast, from this angle apparently boring into the clouds, but when I looked down, wary about letting my attention wander from details of wind and tiller for more than a few seconds, I could see water in the bottom of the boat where no water should be. Not another leak!

Oh, there was David Hirtle, rowing stolidly towards the shore in his double-ended yellow dory. I'd been thinking about them, David and his mother Evangeline. I edged the tiller over slightly to narrow the gap between the two boats and called across the water, "Hello, David, how are you?"

"Hullo, Miz -us Wattss," he replied in his slow monotone, making four words out of the three-word greeting.

"How've you been?" But he didn't reply and I watched the bent back with the strong shoulders and the bowed head recede as he rowed doggedly in toward the cove where the mailboxes stood, stiff iron sentinels on the rocks at shore's edge, each with its square mouth securely locked. Why they needed to lock the mail boxes on these small islands where everyone was related to everyone else I didn't know. "Good fences make good neighbors?"

Funny old David. Not really old actually. In fact it was hard to say how old he was; he walked, talked—rowed—like an old man, heavy slow movements like the loud and careful one-note tones and deliberate pacing of his speech. But he couldn't be much over twenty; I could remember when he used to come out to the house as a boy. I planned to ask Garnet Rinehardt, when I saw her.

As the sailboat slipped through the water, the yellow dory slowly grew smaller before it disappeared around the point of rocks in the cove. I remembered previous summers, when David had rowed out to visit. Sometimes he'd play cards with the children, if the game was a simple one, and sometimes I'd offer him a beer while he sat squarely upright in one of the kitchen chairs, offering no information but answering questions patiently.

"How was the winter, David?"

"Not too bad Missus Watts,"

I remembered one of those conversations vividly. "Do you read comics, David?"

"Nope." A long pause. "I cain't read at'all." And then a piece of information for once, offered voluntarily, "Daddy cain't read neither."

"Do you watch TV?"

"Yup, we know all them stories."

Oh, the soap operas. "Which do you like best?"

"We like 'em all. The tube burned out last year but we watch 'em all and we knowed all the people."

I had a quick, astonishing image of the three of them in that grubby, junk littered kitchen, chairs pulled up to the TV, eyes fixed on the blank screen, listening to the pictures.

David wore his fishing boots everywhere, usually still flecked with fish scales and blood from the morning's catch, and, to be honest, one didn't want to speculate on how recently any of his clothes had been changed. It was just as well to keep the door open during his visits. He was getting to be a bit of problem as he grew older. I'd met him once, outside of the harbor, rowing toward home in a thick fog. Neither of us should have been so far out, but I supposed he went wherever he chose.

Undoubtedly, he came around the house when we were gone. Once he'd "borrowed" a shovel over the winter, but it was returned, so perhaps the mental quotation marks were unfair.

He was strong too, as a man would be who's pulled up nets and carried stove wood all his life, working alongside his father ever since they'd brought David back from the Home for the Retarded, lonely for the only child they'd never had.

Should one be afraid of David? There were island stories, allusions to a bit of mischief here, lies he'd told, talk about a murderous rage slow to kindle but hard to put out, drinking…but stories feed on stories and grow in the telling. He seemed harmless enough.

"Mummy, where are you going?"

Oops, I'd been diverted by these musings and the boat was veering off. "Just saying good morning to Round Island," I said cheerfully and pushed the tiller over. "Ready about, hard-a-lee," and we scrambled to the other side as the boat turned trimly on her keel, and began slicing back toward the shore.

"I'll drop you off at the shop and you can walk around by the mailboxes and meet me at Garnet's." I figured it would take a good 45 minutes to walk around the shore. "Ok? Don't forget to check the mail." Our box was the only one that wasn't locked.

The two girls grinned at each other—they had secrets of their own—and nodded agreement. I was looking forward to a visit with Garnet, to hearing the winter news. It would begin with weather, storms, the state of the fishing, and the price of lobsters. Then it would move to aches and pains: "How's your arthritis, Garnet?", and then slowly come around to tales based on island feuds and friendships. I'd ask Garnet about the Hirtles, how David and his mother were making out since his father, Lee Hirtle, died.

How I valued these friendships with the fishermen and their families! When the Americans came as summer people we'd been welcomed in like family, adopted in a sense. I was familiar with the customary estrangements and uneasy truces that developed between people "from away" and "locals," but here I felt no hostility, no distance. I remembered the time I'd given one of the fishermen a lift into town. He'd run into a friend and in the course of the conversation the friend said, "Do you have any Americans down there?" The fisherman had replied with pride, "Yup, we got seven ministers and one carpenter."

"We got..." There was the pride of proprietorship in it. The fishermen were the experts with their superior knowledge of boats and the sea; they helped out with house and boat repairs and refused compensation; they offered stories and lunch—a meal defined more by its size than time of day—and the honor of "a bit of rum." I felt privileged to be so hospitably invited into another culture. Oh, yes, they spoke the same language—or almost—but it was like a step back in time, to a world heretofore known only from books, a time just disappearing here when people lived close to the land and made their living from the sea. Their experiences were so different from mine, and their perceptions too, sometimes.

The boat slipped neatly up to the dock—not a bad landing at all—and the girls spilled out. On shore I could see the Hirtle's house, as bright and gleaming a yellow as their dory. Probably the same paint. Sunflower yellow it would be called on the paint chart, or perhaps sunshine gold? The inside of the house, I knew, was quite a different color and complexion. I'd picked my way more than once through a year's trash—boxes, old clothes, empty tin cats, dirty cat dishes, fish bones, soiled newspapers—to win entrance to the kitchen. It was one of those households where if you wanted to use a plate you picked it out of the pile of dirty dishes and washed it first.

David's father had been the one who held the family together, gentle and unassuming like so many of the fisherman. I wondered what would become of them since Lee died suddenly in the winter—pneumonia, was it?

Safely docked, greeted, and hugged at Garnet's, I settled comfortably in the kitchen rocking chair and eventually the conversation moved to local news. "What's happening with David and Evangeline?"

I was surprised by the vehemence of Garnet's response. Evangeline couldn't manage him any more, since Lee died. The two of them were always drinking. They yelled and shouted at each other in the yard. Last night, for example, they'd hired a taxi and gone up to town and when they came back, after midnight, they were both so drunk they couldn't find their way home. You could hear them shouting at each other out on the water. Percy Baker had to go out in his boat and get them off Round Island. She didn't know what would become of them. They should have left David up there at The Home.

Evangeline was an island scandal, an embarrassment. Her slovenly housekeeping, her bad language, and gross appearance were all grist to righteous indignation. She was a great gossip, jovial enough when sober; it was easier to be disapproving when out of her presence. She kept her ear to the party line and her nose to the wind—perfect qualifications for the local newspaper correspondent, though what appeared in the Island News column was often a surprise to the people mentioned.

Garnet was going on: how could people act like that, living in such filth.... And these drinking binges....

There was a knock at the door, but without waiting for a response the door flew open. Rebecca, white-faced and gasping for breath, ran into the room, "Oh, Mummy, Mummy, David Hirtle's drowned."

"But Rebecca, that's not possible!" I reached out for the trembling child. "We just passed him, rowing into the cove." My mind raced between possibilities, incredulity and horror in harness. It was impossible. Not on such a fine day. They had just seen him, spoken to him. But Rebecca's fright was real. I held the firm young body close and felt her shaking. "What happened? Where is he?" And then remembering, "Where's Elianna?"

Elianna herself appeared at the door; clearly she had been running behind.

"I don't know how it happened." Rebecca was crying now, speaking in jerks between sobs but giving herself up to the comforting arms as well. "We looked for the mail, and then we walked past black Hirtle's and Hazel was crying and she said David was 'drownded' and his boat was just drifting around in the cove."

"Well, isn't anybody doing anything?" Action would be a relief. I started toward the door, my arm still round Rebecca, to run down there, to fish him out: a fleeting vision of giving artificial respiration to that sodden drunken body—would he vomit when he came to? Hastily, I pushed the repulsive image below the whirlwind of thoughts fluttering about in my head, and turned to Garnet, who was standing transfixed by the stove, the teakettle still in her hand. "It was bound to happen someday," I said slowly, and then, "We were just talking about him." Had they been Catholic they would have crossed themselves.

I continued toward the door. "We'll go see what we can do," I said to the unmoving Garnet. And then I was outside, walking rapidly with a child on either side, until the path narrowed and we had to walk Indian file, pushing through the high grasses and wild rose bushes or stepping from stone to stone where the hungry tide had come in to take a bite. As we came over the hill, we could see into the little Bell Island cove almost enclosed by land, where many of the early fishermen had built their houses, seeking what shelter they could find from winter storms. Outcroppings of rock on either side stretched fingers toward each other, leaving only a narrow opening for the fishing boats to slip through. On the height of land across the cove I could see the small white church, its spire just rising above the competing spires of spruces, and below it, the humbler wooden building which had been the island school in more prosperous days. Now, on this side of the cove, we could see the house we were hurrying toward, shining with fresh black paint. The old cape was set back, like most of the houses in the cove, perhaps thirty feet from the shore.

The gear for eight men fishing filled the yard and overflowed from the small building by the dock, the fish store. Piles of brightly painted buoys, nets drying on low clothesline arrangements, huge stock piles of lobster traps, grapnels and line: there seemed to be an inexhaustible supply of fishing gear, trade, tackle and trim.

There was no activity in the little cove. The water lay below them, calm and unruffled, a summer's blue. It was a perfect day, a fair day in June. On the far shore, above the rock and flower-filled hillside nestled the bright blue house with the white railed porch where another family of Hirtles lived. I had long ago given up the task of sorting out the relationships between them. Cousins married cousins, brothers of one family married sisters of another. It was all too complicated, but the fact remained that among the 17 families on the islands now there were only four different surnames, all of German origin.

I could see Kathleen Hirtle up there on the porch, looking across at them. Closer now, I saw the yellow dory, gently held in a back eddy by the sentinel mailboxes, still standing at attention.

But there was no activity. There should be crowds, boats, shouts, rescue attempts. It wasn't possible that a person to whom you'd said hello at 10 should be dead at 11. How could David, who rowed everywhere, in any kind of weather, how could he have drowned in this quiet cove surrounded by his relatives?

At the black Hirtle's house they found Hazel, Percy's daughter, crying, wringing her hands and walking about distractedly. Percy, himself, was standing at the end of the dock, pipe clenched in his teeth, and Buddy, the fat, black dog, continued to jump and bark at the end of his tether, more out of habit than ferocity. "Hazel, what happened?" I put my hand sympathetically on the thin shoulder. How frail the old woman was!

"David done drownded hisself." Hazel managed to sniffle out. "David's gone and fallen out of his boat and you know how he always likes to show off his bottle and he fell out and he can't swim and he's drownded… He stood up in the dory and waved it around, and now he's drownded…" She was interrupted by the sight of a small procession winding around the shore path from the opposite direction. It was Malcom, the shop keeper, leading Evangeline who was weeping loudly as she heaved herself over the rocky path.

"Shouldn't we do something? Is he down there?" I looked furtively at the water. Is there a boat?" But already I felt swept into the pattern of non-action. These other people, closer to David in every way, were making no move toward the water. What could she do? Percy did nothing.

"We're waiting for the Mounties." Hazel offered.

Suddenly I didn't want to be there. The noisy procession, Evangeline wailing and the other two urging her to be calm came closer. There was apparently nothing I could do. There were the two little girls to consider, and, I noticed, the wind was rising. Best to get home before there was too much wind for that leaky boat.

"Hazel, how could it happen?" Hazel continued snuffling, blew her nose, tried ineffectually to quiet the dog, and mumbled, "I dunno. I looked out and were he was, rowin' in, and then I looked again and there wasn't no one there."

"Kathleen, did you see what happened?" The procession had arrived. Malcolm was steering Evangeline, wailing, eyes askew, toward the end of the dock, where she slowly lowered herself so that she could lie down and look into the water.

"I was on the telephone and I saw him come in to the cove, figured he was coming to get the mail or see Percy about something, didn't think no more about it. I saw him stand up in the boat, and then I hung up the phone and when I looked again he wasn't there. The dory was just drifting around so I knew something was wrong and I came out on the porch and Shirley said, David's drowned.'"

"What did you do then?"

"I called the Mounties, and Malcom, and he said he'd bring Evangeline over—he knows her best." There was a pause while the four of them stared at the quiet water and the drifting yellow dory. "It was bound to happen, him drinking all the time."

I called the little girls who, with Evangeline, were also gazing fascinated into the water, though apparently there was nothing to be seen, decided against speaking to the distraught mother, mumbled a few words of sympathy to the two women, and set off up the path to Garnet's where the boat was moored, anxious for home.

Later, Garnet told me that the Mounties did come, roaring up in a small boat with a powerful outboard motor about an hour later. They found David standing bolt upright in the mud of the cove bottom, the water only a foot or two above his head. Of course he couldn't swim, few of the fishermen did. "When I go I want go fast," she'd heard Percy Baker say.

The bright yellow dory had drifted across to the other side of the cove, but no one from the small group of mourners and sightseers who gathered as the news traveled had made any attempt to catch it. In the dory, the Mounties found a half empty bottle of rum and a bailing can.

Once, when they were all still alive, we stopped in the house for a visit. I can't remember why: perhaps to invite David out to play cards with the boys. They were all crammed in together in the sitting room/dining room/kitchen: Lee, Evangeline, David, a German shepherd, and several cats. It was filthy. Cat dishes and cat excrement on the floor, human dishes from the last several meals cluttering the table, some on the floor, along with newspapers, bills, ashtrays, and a discarded sweater. Along one wall was a bed, which served as a couch, facing an iron stove which was both heat source and cooker, a couple of rocking chairs in which sweet mannered Lee rocked incessantly while David held down the other.

I remember going into the house after they were all dead with Olaf McCletchy, who was interested in buying it. The downstairs room was as before only made worse for its emptiness, the upstairs room was unspeakable. One rumpled dirty bed and human excrement in corners, evidence that Evangeline was too troubled to care for a chamber pot or to get herself downstairs. When Olaf came out of the house he took off his shoes and threw them into the ocean.

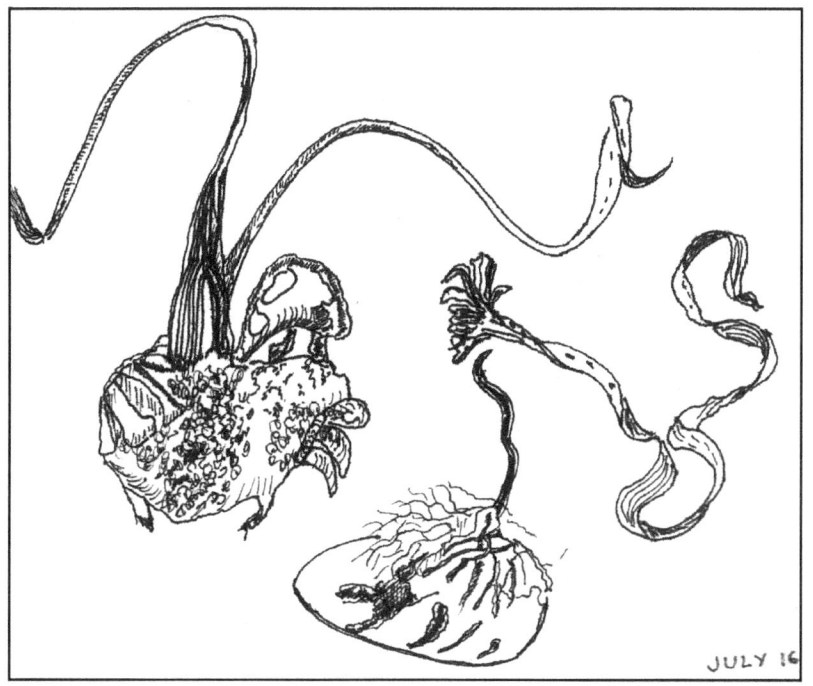

July 16 Findings on Halibut Head Beach

Magic Beach looking north towards Cape LaHave. (Courtesy of Rose Watts.)

ESSAYS

No Trusts Without Trust

Author's note: This was first published by Antioch University in a magazine called *Whole Terrain*.

The LaHave Islands Marine Museum Hall was abuzz with chatter and good-humored laughter when I entered late in August 2013, the sun just setting over the Bell's Island bridge. Some friends and neighbors socialized around the back table eating home-baked cookie squares while others gravitated toward the coffee machine. The Museum Hall is a plain, wood-frame building, small enough to make 20 people look like a crowd and—on this evening—a cheerful one. In addition to the nine or ten Americans present who had been coming to the islands every summer for over forty years and a few more recent summer people, there were two fishermen who could trace their families back to the first settlers in the mid-1800s, and one retired local businessman.

My family and I had purchased a small house on the islands in 1968 as part of a first wave of summer residents. We knew the local fishermen and their families well. They had welcomed us when we first came, and again each summer; they taught us how to fish, and rescued us from ill-advised sailing adventures. The first Americans were people of modest means. We repaired the houses we bought for so little but did not change the look of the islands, and we felt blessed to be welcomed as "our Americans come home."

I had called the meeting when people asked about the efforts on the part of the Middle Island summer residents to establish a local land trust. We had no legal obligation to inform anyone of our intentions but an open meeting was consistent with our desire to share local resources and do what was good for the land, the community, and the future.

There were many obstacles to this land trust, some financial, some legal. But the biggest obstacle was totally unanticipated: the negative reaction of the local long-term residents to the establishment of a "Preservation Society." This essay shares the conflicting values, assumptions about sustainability, community ties, and opinions about the environment and the fate of the planet.

The LaHave Islands Preservation Society (LIPS) was conceived as a way to preserve certain plots of land on the LaHave Islands from any further development and to hold them in trust for public use. Specifically, we had the opportunity to buy what we called Magic Beach, a stretch perhaps 500 feet long, facing the open sea but protected by islands on either side. Behind the beach was a freshwater pond surrounded by cattails, wetlands, and a stand of hemlocks, spruce, and small deciduous trees.

Common land is not a new concept in the LaHave Islands, which comprise approximately 25 small islands and one large island, Cape LaHave, the first land sighted by Champlain when he came upon the New World. The Cape has long sand beaches, woodlands, ponds, creeks, a grassy head looking out to sea, and a deep bay, a perfect hatchery for fish and other marine life. It has never been lived on but that does not mean never used. From the time they first settled the islands, the fishermen collected materials for their traps from the Cape, grazed cows, and planted potatoes. In winter they collected firewood there, walking oxen over the ice to bring it home. This common became the property of the municipality of Lunenburg in the 1970s.

Magic Beach, the one we were hoping to preserve, is on Middle Island, also a place of natural beauty, its value enhanced by the presence of Cape LaHave. Since the Cape and a few small islands were already conserved as common land, part of another small island would only be an extension of what already existed. Magic Beach was owned by fellow Americans who were willing to sell it at the price they paid in 1996 if we wanted to create a trust to protect it for public use.

When we first came to the islands, about a century after they were first settled, fishing was changing. Two-way radios and radar made it safer. Government subsidies made fishing life more secure. Sails gave way to motors. The fishermen and their families, no longer so dependent on proximity to the fishing grounds, moved back to the mainland with its schools and shops and hospitals, leaving empty houses and land reverting to its natural state.

At the same time, quietly and quickly, fishing itself disappeared. Draggers from as close as the U.S. and as far as Japan moved into the North Atlantic and stripped the ocean bottom. One of the world's great resources was destroyed in less than 50 years and with it went the remainder of the fishing community. In 1920 there were ten houses on Middle Island. By 1964 there were four, only two inhabited. It was the same on other islands: empty houses, crumbling foundations, no lights. Through the 1980s and 90s some lots were sold to Germans, Canadians, and Americans. Property taxes doubled. Large wood and glass houses appeared on the headlands, "No trespassing" signs sprang up, and the freedom of the beaches, the uninterrupted shore lines, the modest fishermen's cottages, and the old-time character of the islands was disappearing.

In an attempt to preserve some of the culture and natural space we cherished about these islands, we contacted the local office of the Canadian Nature Conservancy. Craig Smith came out to the islands, walked the beach, surveyed the pond, wetlands, and three old house sites, and proclaimed Magic Beach worthy of preservation. He warned us of the obstacles to setting up a society as Americans in Canada. The land would have to be purchased at present market value. The capital gains tax would be 20 percent of the assessed market value, regardless of what we paid. The financial hurdles seemed impossible. We thanked him and put the idea aside. But it didn't go away.

Up the shore from us, the Kingsburg Coastal Conservancy (KCC) had the same concerns for Hirtle Beach, which was quickly becoming overrun with large homes. In 2010, we talked to some board members and they invited us to come in under their umbrella and to draw on their experience. They were working through the problems of charitable giving with accompanying tax relief and they had the expertise we did not; however, we soon realized that the KCC was a very active, well-publicized organization and we had a small semi-private beach with less than 14 acres of field and wetland. We could imagine fleets of small boats converging on Magic Beach, more than enough to destroy the land and relative solitude we were trying to protect. The plan changed again.

At this point, David Seamen, the son of one of the first Americans on the islands, now a member of an accounting firm in New York City, offered to help. He understood legal documents, lawyer talk, and finances, and was generous with his time and financial help. We worked through our concerns and our friend spent the next two years talking with a lawyer, drawing up articles of incorporation, by-laws, and a memorandum of understanding. The mission for the LaHave Islands Preservation Society was "to protect and conserve islands, undeveloped land, wetland, lands of importance for ecological or aesthetic reasons, farmland, marine areas, scenic areas, and historic landscapes, specifically Magic Beach."

The statement also stressed our intention "To promote awareness of the need for rated coastal and marine management, to facilitate beneficial management actions, and to mitigate coastal and marine degradation."

With a comprehensive memorandum of understanding and by-laws in hand, we needed to form a board of trustees, at least half of them Canadians, and we could begin the legal formalities for becoming a Canadian nonprofit conservancy. Once approved, there would still be work to do: raising money to buy the land, working through issues of tax relief and insurance, and establishing guidelines for maintenance of the area, but these seemed manageable now that we had a clear sense of direction. With obstacles overcome after six years of negotiations, we were prepared to nominate board members and move ahead. That's when I announced the public meeting on Aug. 23, 2013.

The backlash was immediate. The three local men signaled distrust by their stance and questions at the open meeting, then made it clear in conversations with their neighbors that they harbored strong suspicions about the project. By the following morning calls and emails were coming in. Our plan, and perhaps our presentation, called up recent and long-standing grievances, like a magnet picking up shards. Most of the objections revealed significant differences in our perceptions, both social and environmental. Some neighbors expressed concern that Americans would be making decisions and controlling Canadian land. Others remembered an attempt to make Cape LaHave a national park and how it divided the islanders.

"We have always been able to fish off those shores, to land and to hunt, and now we will not be able to do so," said one man. "Even if you say we will, what happens when someone else, in 20 years, is making the rules?"

Others worried about the financial impact on their properties: "The conservation efforts to the north and south of us, like the Kingsburg Conservancy, have just resulted in higher property values and more and more people moving in and privatizing the land." Some expressed worry about land access, fearing what happened at nearby Cherry Hill when beach access was denied to save the piping plovers. Loud and clear we heard: "What's wrong with just leaving things the way they are?"

Several objections revealed misunderstandings about the protections guaranteed in the bylaws and about the process of setting up a preservation trust. For example, hunting, fishing, and picnicking by the public were specifically protected, and more Canadians than Americans would be making the decisions. We might have countered each objection with an explanation, but the real problem appeared to be a lack of trust. The fishermen did not trust us—the summer residents—to abide by these guidelines, and they did not trust us to understand or care about their concerns.

Some concerns were legitimate. Property values did increase near conservation land, and less land was available to buy. Areas were permanently closed to preserve the fish, birds, or plants. None of the concerns addressed the issue of conservation, or the shelf life of species when their habitat is degraded, even though these fishermen were deeply affected by the end of the fishing industry due to ecological losses.

What was not articulated, but seemed to be implicit, was a difference in values, driven in part by the difference in perceptions. In *The Environmental Case*, a collection of case studies about environmental conflicts, Judith Layzer writes: "Environmental policy disputes almost always concern fundamental differences in values and...the way problems are defined and solutions depicted plays a central role in shaping how those values get translated into policies."

When we framed the problem as an "us" and "them" scenario, "they" were not making a connection between the death of the fisheries and the looming death of piping plovers, starfish, wetlands, and sphagnum moss, or the loss of common land for recreational purposes. The reality is that both sides care deeply about the ecology of the islands. Unfortunately, one side has a possible small-scale solution while the other sees the solution as part of the threat. By identifying the values we hold in common, we might be able to define the problems and imagine solutions together.

Within a week of the August meeting, we decided to again place on hold the plan to create a preservation society on the LaHave Islands until we could figure out how to frame the problems and describe solutions in a way that would bring us together, rather than widen the separation. It was clear that proceeding with the plans would be a direct affront to the people who had lived on the islands for generations.

Magic Beach will have to wait again while we address the education and advocacy elements of our mission statement. We will begin by defining the problems and searching for the solutions together—in the Museum Hall, and on the wharf. We must find common ground if we wish to preserve land for common use. In order to create a trust we first have to build trust.

Nelson Hirtle bringing some fish from his catch to Middle Island.

Who Hears the Fishes When They Cry?

Who knows what admirable virtue of fishes may be below the low-water-mark, bearing up against a hard destiny, not admired by that lone creature who can appreciate it! Who hears the fishes when they cry?

– Henry David Thoreau

It was a fair morning in June, the sea a calm cerulean blue, sparkling in the reflected sunlight. A few terns plummeted head first in the water and came up with something small and silvery wiggling on the end of the beak, and in the woods behind the house a song sparrow cranked up for the trill. I was cranking up the wood stove for breakfast and the children were stirring in the back bedroom. Out the kitchen window I could see the fishing boats coming in, a working man's regatta of white and brightly painted Cape Island and double-ended fishing boats. The seagulls swirled above them in patterns of calligraphy washed across the cloudless morning sky and added their cries to the sound of the motors, the swoosh of the parting waters.

Dimly, crawling up out of sleep, I'd heard the boats going out around 4 a.m., at that hour a chorus of motor made purrs, growls and putt-putts. Each wife could tell the sound of her husband's motor and could identify most of the others along the shore. "Oh, that's Leon coming in now. Must have had a good catch," Kathleen Hirtle might say without rising from her chair to look out the window.

This morning, a white boat with green trim broke out of the flotilla and began steaming toward our cove, the swirl of complaining gulls drawn along by invisible ties. It was Kathleen's husband, Collin and his son, Wade. Because the tide was high, the boat came right up to the dock, both men leaning over the side and grinning as the children spilled out of the house and raced to the shore. "T'ought you might like a nice mess a'mackerel for breakfast," Collin said, his lined, brown face still creased in a smile, as he brought out six newly dressed mackerel and laid them on the dock, their iridescent rose, black and silvery sides echoing the shine on the water.

My husband, not to be outdone in courtesy, invited Collin and Wade up to the house, but when they grinned again, pointing to their blood- and scale-flecked oilskin overalls he sent one of the children for a few bottles of beer and squatted down on the dock for a "visit" while I gathered up the mackerel and went back to the stove.

Collin's great grandfather emigrated to Nova Scotia from Germany in the early part of the 19th century and his grandparents were among the first settlers on these islands in the mouth of the LaHave River. For a hundred years a few families, fleeing the poor harvests of Germany, Scotland and Ireland gradually settled along the coast and then moved to the islands, adding houses as the sons grew up, married, and started families of their own. The life was hard but land was readily available and the fruits of the sea seemed infinite.

From the turn of the century until the mid-1950s, more or less, the fishing communities on the islands grew and prospered. In the beginning men sailed or rowed to the fishing grounds and so houses were built on the islands furthest out to sea. The women managed the house, the garden and farm animals, wood gathering and water carrying, the children and all the necessary back-up for the men who went out fishing no matter the weather. Fishing, in that era, meant either off-shore fishing: you went out daily before dawn in your own boat, with probably a son or nephew aboard, and dropped nets or jigged for the fish prevalent at that time of year and in those waters. The other way to fish was to go off in the big boats, and fish from dories in the fish rich waters of the Grand Banks or Georges Bank.

An alternative was to go on the schooners to the West Indies, trading salt cod and lumber for rum, sugar and dynamite. The cleared and cultivated land became more productive. Sails gave way to the single cylinder engine, then the double cylinder, then the car engine and finally the marine engine.

We came to the LaHave islands in 1968, not much more than 100 years after the first settlers, but we came only as summer people to live in the houses now abandoned by fishermen. We were welcomed into the community like family. "When are you coming home?" they'd ask us when we left in the fall. We learned from them about the local waters, the ways of the weather, where to fish for mackerel and how to cook an eel. Best of all, perhaps, were the yarns about being shipwrecked in the south seas, submarined in the first world war, near escapes at sea and eccentric neighbors.

In the 1960s it was no lack of fish that emptied the outer islands; it was better fishing boats and equipment. With motors and safety equipment in the boats fishermen could live on the islands or move to the mainland with electricity, telephones, cars and more convenient access to schools and hospitals. They could sail farther out and be more certain of coming home. Although each generation had been better off than the previous one, this generation benefited the most from improving technology, and more substantial government support in the form of subsidies for fishing gear, unemployment, free medical care and pensions. In 1968 technological improvements had made a significant difference in the lives of the fisherman without disturbing the balance in sustainable practices.

In our first ten years on the island, fish were plentiful. We could row out into the sea, drop a jig line and come back within the hour with cod or mackerel for supper. The kids fished for flounder off the docks, dug clams on nearby beaches, and mussels, which the fishermen spurned, could be torn off the rocks for as large a meal as you wished. Some days the boats came in so loaded the gunwales were almost awash and only the white wake would be visible at the stern. In June there were salmon for those with licenses, but the staples were herring, cod, mackerel, and haddock. Sometimes the men caught ground fish—flounder and halibut, sometimes perch but always cod.

For a few years the squid came in and we had a glorious time dipping jigs, sticks, old brooms, whatever into the water and pulling them up again a few minutes later with squid hanging from every surface, squirting black ink, making a colossal, hilarious mess. Once one of the younger fishermen came in with a 4-foot shark that had got caught in his net and we cut it up then and there on the dock. It was delicious.

Between our arrival in 1968 and 1998, the fish disappeared. From abundance to scarcity in 30 years. "The culprit—as it almost always has been in fishing—was a sudden change in technology," Sebastian Junger, in "The Perfect Storm" goes on to explain: "fishing had changed, boats were using satellite navigation, electronic fish finders, temperature depth gauges. Radar reflectors were used to track gear and new monofilament made it possible to set 30 or 40 miles of line at a time."

He quotes a government study of the 1980s that said, "The technological change appears to be bumping up against the limits of the resource."

Large trawlers scoured the bottom, with nets and huge chains, sometimes two or three abreast, bringing up literally tons of fish. They picked out the few fish which were marketable and dropped the remainder back, dead. They "raked the bottom so hard that they actually leveled outcrops and filled in valleys—the very habitats where fish thrived."

By the 1980s, "haddock landings had plummeted to one-fiftieth of what they were in 1960, cod landings had dropped by a factor of four. New quick-freeze techniques allowed boats to work halfway around the world and process their fish as they went. Enormous Russian factory ships put to sea for months at a time and scoured the bottom with nets that could take thirty tons of fish in a single haul. They fished practically within sight of the American coast, and within years the fish populations had been staggered by 50 percent losses."

The American response was to announce a 200-mile offshore limit to American sovereignty, and then hastily set to work constructing ships which could do the same thing.

"Better equipment resulted in such huge takes that prices dropped and fishermen had to resort to more and more devastating methods just to keep up."

Fishing on shore for a living is no longer viable along most of the north Atlantic coast. Every year there are fewer fish and, at last, more restrictions. Whether it will be possible to restore the greed devastated stocks is still unknown. Whether it will be possible to learn from the experience is still unknown. Possibly not. I read now that marine scientists are predicting for shellfish in Newfoundland a fate similar to that of the cod if the current rate of take continues, but every effort to regulate the industry is defeated.

During our brief 30-plus years on the island there has also been a sudden and startling drop in tide line creatures and in song birds. In just the last ten years we have noted the almost complete disappearance of sea urchins, star fish, mussels, and sand dollars. Few periwinkles crust the dock pilings. There has been a corresponding decline in the number of song birds. The swallows which used to make a nuisance of themselves nesting in the barn, the warblers teasing us with song but never staying still long enough to be identified: at least 20 species I recorded in the early years I am unable to find now.

Whether the destruction of the sea's bottom and the corresponding interruptions in the food chain are responsible for the disappearance of the tide line creatures I do not know. To what extent increasing urbanization and chemical additives in the environment are responsible for the decreasing activity in our woods I do not know. I do know that, as each summer when I return to the islands I realize that one more bird is absent, one more sea creature gone, one more fisherman has moved away I feel the reality of "endangered species" and "silent spring" not as mere concepts but as personal loss.

This essay is not to rant against change. It is not a condemnation of technology. Safer boats and better living conditions make sense. However, throwing back 90 percent of the catch and leveling the ocean bottom makes no sense. Building more and bigger draggers when the fish stocks are plummeting makes no sense. It is about acknowledging those times when "technological change bumps up against the limits of the resource," and putting on the brakes, practicing restraint, passing and enforcing regulations to conserve the resource, whether it be cod fish, shell fish, wood or oil. This essay is against greed; against those who cannot say enough is enough; against action without consideration for the long-term consequences; against continuing with a practice even when the long term consequences are known to be disastrous; against the terrible disrespect we show for living things and the earth we have been given.

No fish, no terns, no fishermen, no fishing community. The fish and birds are not the only casualties of technology coupled with self-interest. Collin is dead and Wade is working at a hospital in town. There are only two or three elderly men fishing off the islands now where once there were 30–40.

The older men die or retire, their sons have gone elsewhere for work or now live on government subsidies. There are no fishermen's wives rocking by the window. Their empty houses are being snapped up at startling prices by summer folk, mostly non-resident, mostly non-Canadian.

Perhaps the changes in the LaHave Islands fishing community were inevitable as families moved off island and became absorbed into the mainstream of late 20th century North America. Perhaps there was no way to stop the advance of civilization in which the TV replaces personal story telling and well packaged, well-advertised food replaces your home grown or sea caught dinner. Perhaps the advantages of electricity and, even more important, the access to social services are worth the losses, but I mourn them nonetheless.

This essay is about loss but it is also about celebration and gratitude. Like the death of a friend I mourn the loss of the terns and the cod; like the death of a family I mourn the loss of my fishing community.

Even more than the loss of a resource our lives on the island, all our lives are lessened and diminished by the disappearance of these living creatures and different cultures. All the more reason, then, to be grateful for the opportunity we had to enjoy them in the fullness of their time, and to be grateful for what remains. I still have the ubiquitous sea gulls screaming overhead or swimming upright and regal in the blue morning cove; there are still song sparrows in the hemlock tree and crabs scuttling in the waving seaweed. We can celebrate, we can be grateful for what was and what remains, but we must redouble our efforts, every one of us, to preserve what is still preservable and to attempt to restore what we have destroyed. We must add our voices to the cry of the fishes.

"Writing for me is both anthropology and archeology: digging through the artifacts, cherishing the human history from the past and in the present." Heidi Watts, Middle Island, 2021.

EPILOGUE

> Why Write? Why Write about this time, these islands, these people? —November 2021

Good questions. I wrote about the 50 plus years our family spent the summer months on the LaHave Islands off the eastern coast of Nova Scotia because I wanted to record my personal experience with a fishing community for the second half of the 20th century "up close and personal." I wanted to record what I was learning about small, isolated communities built around a natural resource dying before our eyes; about a community in obvious transition, with the spread of telephone access, and then one technical innovation tumbling in after the other. For the fishermen, this meant major changes in safety protections from the off-shore radio to radar (also good for finding fish), and on the other side, great change in the social safety net: government pensions, unemployment, accessible health services, and much more.

   I wanted to shine a flashlight on our indifference to our responsibilities for the gifts of the planet, I wanted to show just how much a community built around a natural resource can die as the resource is used up or becomes unavailable. I wanted to catch a moment in time that I was a part of and at the same time only an observer.

   But that is not the only reason for writing, of course. For myself, my family and our neighbors I wanted to catch and hold as many characteristics of the time, the place and the people as I could. And that too is not the only reason. I wanted to know more about what I was feeling, or seeing, thinking or doing. When you get right down to it, why does anyone write?

   We asked our neighbor, John Irving, who had just published his first novel, why he wrote and he said, "I had had some experiences and I wanted to know what I thought of them."

John Dewey, I think it is, said, "Experience is not what happens to you: it's what you do with the experience that matters," and I am told E.M. Forster said, "How do I know what I think until I see what I wrote?"

In short, for some people writing is a way of reflecting, a way of organizing and prioritizing thoughts, another way to access intuitive understanding for reconsideration or for sharing thoughts and observations. Writing puts a little distance between me and my first perception, or me and strong emotion which helps with getting some detachment. Wordsworth or Coleridge, one of those romantics, talked about "emotion recollected in tranquility."

However, writing is not the only avenue to detachment or reflection. For some people speaking, sharing, putting those thoughts out verbally accrues the same value and perhaps for others the expression and self realization comes with making art. I would not say that writing is the best way to know what one is thinking, but it is so for me. The writing I did, recording fishermen's voices, trying to see above or below or beyond the immediate impressions, sharing their stories and my experiences with other people and with the principal actors did help me to see—and to better appreciate—the extent of the environmental disasters, but also the warmth and idyiosyncracies of a very special community over fifty years. Writing for me is both anthropology and archeology: digging through the artifacts, cherishing the human history from the past and in the present.

July 22 Full Moon from From Bedroom Window

Acknowledgements

This project is like a three-legged stool. There is a writer, an artist and a producer. The producer is my son, Richard. If it were not for Richard this book would not be in your hands right now. And were it not for the drawings of seaweed, trees and sunsets from Linda Rubinstein it would be only one third of what it is.

Last year, as I was slowly disentangling myself from most of my commitments, professional and volunteer, Richard suggested we create a book out of some of the material he was posting on a blog for me (www.heidiwatts.blogspot). He would take care of all the arrangements: finding a publisher, merging the separate moving parts into a whole, and I would only have to do the selection, fill in the gaps, and hand it on to him. His constant refrain: "The perfect is the enemy of the good" carried me into the project, around, through and out.

Linda, and her husband Chip, have been faithful Middle Island devotees for over thirty years, "like family", as they say on the islands. When they come for their annual summer visit Chip repairs everything in sight while Linda draws and paints.

Heidi Watts

A Note About Illustrations

Drawings for this book are the work of Linda Rubinstein, from *The Book of Days* (2014), and *Glorious Light-Nova Scotia Sunsets* (2015); both artist books.

Unless noted otherwise, any photos used in this book are courtesy of the Watts family.

REFERENCES & ENDNOTES

Barss, Peter. 1978. *Images of Lunenburg County*. McClelland & Stewart. Toronto.

DesBrisay, Matthew. 1900. *The History of Lunenburg County*.

Junger, Sebastian. 1997. *The Perfect Storm*. W.W. Norton. New York.

McCloskey, Roberts. 1957. *Time of Wonder*. Viking Press.

Mowat, Farley. 1963. *Never Cry Wolf*. McClelland & Stewart. Toronto.

Peterson, Roger Tory. 1947. *A Field Guide to the Birds of North America, 3rd Edition*. Houghton Mifflin.

Tinbergen, Nicolaas. 1953. *The Herring Gulls World*. Collins. London.

Tinbergen, Nicolaas. 1951. *The Study of Instinct*. Clarendon Press. Oxford.

Watts, Heidi. 2006. "Who Hears the Fishes When They Cry?." *Whole Terrain*. Antioch New England.

Watts, Heidi. 2017. "No Trusts Without Trust." *Whole Terrain*. Antioch New England.

Watts, Heidi. 2022. "Communists, Aliens, and Pacifists, go home!" *Heidi Watts, www.heidiwatts.blogspot.com*.

Watts, Simon. 2010. *A Nova Scotia Calendar*. SW Publishing.

www.ingramcontent.com/pod-product-compliance
Lightning Source LLC
Chambersburg PA
CBHW051607170426
43196CB00038B/2957